Cancale

Baie de Beaussais

Cap Fréhel

Sables
d'Or-les-Pins

Din...

ingamp

N12

ST. BRIEUC

Quintin

Rance
Estuary

DINAN

S D'ARMOR

N12

FOUGÈRES

Loudéac

N164

RENNES

Forêt Domaniale
de Rennes

VITRÉ

vy

Forêt Domaniale
de Paimpont

A81

D766

N24

Paimpont

Ploërmel

MORBIHAN

Pays de
Vilaine

Landes de
Lanvaux

Auray

VANNES

Rochefort-en-Terre

Châteaubriant

Redon

La Roche-Bernard

eron

LOIRE
ATLANTIQUE

Herbignac

A11

Golfe du
Morbihan

ST. NAZAIRE

NANTES

l'Ile aux Pies
et le Grand Site Naturel
de la Vallée l'Oust

The Nature
of France

BRITTANY

The Nature
of France

BRITTANY

Dennis & Ann
Furnell

PALLAS ATHENE

Contents

For David – resolute Francophile. With our appreciation for his support and encouragement, for his imaginative Christmas and birthday presents without which our cellar would be less well stocked and our knowledge of viticulture less informed. And our evening walks less pleasurably punctuated.

Violet Helleborine (Epipactis purpurata)*: An uncommon woodland orchid often found growing in shady beech woods. The pollinating insects (wood wasps) are drawn to the narcotic nectar*

SWAROVSKI

O P T I K

Special thanks go to John Brinkley of Swarovski Optik UK and Gerold Dobler and Gerhard Swarovski of Swarovski Optik KG. John was particularly helpful in supplying some fine optical equipment and also providing essential support in the early stages of planning – without which we might not have even begun this project. And he was more than happy to accompany us on oyster tasting expeditions to France.

Breeding over much of the coastal fringe and estuaries of Brittany, the redshank announces its presence with white flashing wing bars and a sharp piping call

Foreword
by Betty Beningfield

When Dennis and Ann Furnell invited me to join them on a wildlife holiday in Brittany I welcomed the opportunity. I'd never visited this part of France before and to go touring around the countryside with friends that know the area so well would be, I knew, an experience not to be missed.

St Malo was our port of arrival, and within the walls of this beautiful city there is a fascinating history, as we learned when we took a ride on the little tourist train. We also pottered about the narrow streets looking in the shop windows and bought some Crème Brûlée dishes, an essential purchase as we had begun an appraisal on this delicious dessert of English origin (Burnt Cream) that the French have made their own. We tasted Crème Brûlée throughout Brittany, but the one we ate in an open-air café overlooking the square in St Malo was the best. From Dennis' point of view, however, Cancale was a dream come true, with as much seafood as anyone could wish – especially oysters. The sea front at Cancale is lined with seafood restaurants – dozens of them.

As one would expect in France the food was consistently good and we enjoyed memorable meals in many delightful settings. At St. Malo there was an old-fashioned-looking hotel

Southern marsh orchid (Dactylorhiza praetermissa): *Grows on lime-rich marshland, particularly in the lee of old sand dunes*

nestling under the walls, looking for all the world like something out of the television series "Allo 'Allo'. And at Bénodet we enjoyed the hospitality of Monsieur and Madame Erwin Clément at the Hôtel Armoric.

From a wildlife point of view, it's difficult to know where to start. There is simply so much to see. One of my favourite places was Kermor Plage, a few miles along the coast from Bénodet, with miles and miles of wide sandy beaches (if there were more than half a dozen people we thought it was crowded). We spent an afternoon collecting shells and exploring the dunes and nature reserve backing the beach. We delighted in the birds, butterflies and wildflowers on the headlands, laughed at the frogs' chorus and ended the day listening enthralled to two local choirs singing traditional and classical songs in the church at Plobannalec.

It's lucky that Dennis is so observant, otherwise when we stopped for a picnic in the Forêt de Carnoët near Quimperlé we might have missed a tawny owl trying desperately to make itself invisible in the mid afternoon sunlight against the trunk of a Scots pine and a beautiful demoiselle dragonfly flitting up and down the woodland ride.

In central Brittany we discovered the Forêt Domaniale de Paimpont (more romantically known as the forest of Brocéliande) – a place of Arthurian legend, full of giant megaliths and the remains of ancient dwellings. We came across a young man eerily playing a didjeridu. It was magical to find Merlin's Tomb and fun to search for the Fountain of Youth. Mont St Michel, surrounded by the sea, is a fairy-tale place. It's a steep climb to the monastery at the top, but I'm glad I made it. You can see for miles around and when the tide recedes,

Man orchid (Aceras anthropophorum): *A strange plant belonging to the group of insect-pollinated orchids. The insect pollinator is not known, but may be one of the feather-winged moths. Plant found on limestone and lime-rich grassland*

flocks of sheep graze the salt marsh. The meat is a local speciality; indeed it's famous throughout the whole of France and known as *Pré Salé*.

We visited walled cities with typical French markets and watched street entertainers and fire-eaters, took a boat trip up the lovely river Odet to Quimper and explored the old quarter and the magnificent cathedral. We criss-crossed the region by car with no difficulty at all. Very little traffic, remarkably empty roads, excellent food and an abundance of wildlife – what more could you wish for?

Tawny owl

Preface

France is one of the most popular of holiday destinations. People come for the style, for the fascinating history and, of course, the food and wine. In our case, as well as these delights, we also have a love of the countryside and we have yet to find anywhere in rural France that does not live up to expectations. This book and others in the series *The Nature of France* have been written to share our pleasure in travelling through this beautiful country. Each volume will take a region, and explore it via its subdivisions, the administrative units called *départements*. Brittany, an ancient duchy, is made up of the départements of Côte d'Armor, Finistère, Ille et Vilaine and Morbihan.

We begin the book with an introduction to the region as a whole, and set the scene by describing what it is that has made this part of France so rich in wildlife – from the underlying bedrock, fundamental to the flora and fauna, to the history that has shaped the fields, moorland, marshes and forests that support both people and wildlife.

The four departements follow in alphabetical order with an individual introduction. In each, the history of the landscape, the variety of habitats and the wildlife most likely to be encountered are described in greater detail. Next comes a chapter on the nature reserves and other places of wildlife interest that we ourselves found to be the most rewarding. This is the heart of the book. Naturally, there are many, many more nature

reserves and places of wildlife interest than we have room for here; which, to our way of thinking, is just as it should be, since it leaves you, the reader, the pleasure of discovery.

Each section finishes with a brief description of some of the towns and villages of interest or significance in the departement. And, as this is France we are talking about, there's an introduction to the foods of the region. The French are justifiably proud of their tradition of local produce and speciality dishes.

If you have travelled in Brittany before, you will probably have your own favourite stopping places, but if you are new to the region, we have made a few recommendations – hotels we have stayed in and restaurants where we have eaten which, we feel, have a certain something extra to offer. We have also included a few hints and tips about what to do if you want a change from wildlife-watching – cycling, walking, inland boating and water sports.

Finally, the practical information, which includes, besides the more regular items, a comprehensive list of market days and, naturally, a list of the relevant conservation organisations involved in running the nature reserves and national park.

Bonnes Vacances!

Dennis and Ann Furnell
Hemel Hempstead, Spring 2003

Sow thistle (Sonchus cleraceus) *and poppy* (Papaver rhoeas)*:*
Sow thistle is a common farmland wild plant

The Dartford warbler,
Landes de Lanvaux, Morbihan

Brittany

PARIS

FRANCE

200km

Introduction

Occupying the north-west corner of France, the ancient region of Brittany is made up of four departments – Côtes d'Armor, Finistère, Ille et Vilaine and Morbihan – and covers a land area similar to that of Wales. Over one thousand miles of stunningly beautiful coastline faces both the Atlantic and the English Channel (known to the French as La Manche). For passengers from England on the Western Channel crossings, the first sight of the nature of France is gulls and gannets riding the pressure waves generated by the ferry's urgent progress. A great many birds nest along the Channel coast, on rocky shards like those that make up Les Sept Iles – a scatter of granite buttresses capped by thrifty turf, honeycombed with puffin burrows, edged with hard rocks white-washed by generations of auks and gannets, and exposed to the gales that sweep up the Western Approaches.

The ancient peoples of Brittany are thought to have originated from the south-eastern European and Mediterranean nomadic tribes who exploited the post-Ice Age landscape of Western Europe with its immense herds of game and large herbivores like bison and wild cattle. Gradually these hunter-gatherer peoples settled to a more pastoral way of life and during a period

A Brittany path: the thin heathland soil soon erodes to create permanent paths across the heather and gorse, providing open space where butterflies and sand lizards can sunbathe

of time, from 8,000 to 5,000 years ago, expanded and developed culturally to an astonishing degree. Theirs was a life bound to nature and they left behind a rich legacy of amazingly complex religious and funerary monuments built of stone. Their ability to create such monuments, and the social organisation and cost in time and materials involved in such construction work, point to a highly structured and exceptionally well-organised society. But there are tantalisingly few clues as to the type of dwellings they lived in and finds of artifacts, or mortal remains are extremely rare. They left no written language and no clear cultural information was handed down through the usual path of verbal folklore. What we know for certain is that they worked with bronze and polished stone tools; what is conjectured is the fact that their dwellings were built of wood and have decayed without trace.

These pre-Celtic Europeans would have been the same nomadic tribes that reached Britain and settled into the pastoral society that built Stonehenge and the circles at Avebury in southern England. Yet, for all we know and admire their industry, they remain an enigma. It is as though the ancient Egyptians, having built the pyramids, disappeared from the scene leaving only a few burnt bones, metal tools and delicate earthenware pottery as clues to their social and physical existence. The interior of Brittany is littered with the monuments of these pre-Celts – to such an extent that the region must have offered particular benefits in terms of grazing and raw materials. Even in those far off times there was a thriving trade across the Channel, something that continued when their successors occupied the land. Many fishermen and traders from the western and southern coasts of Britain braved these shores to trade pottery, jewelry, cider, tin and gold (flakes of the sun to the ancient Celts) which was, indeed still is, washed from the sands and gravels of the rivers Aulne, Blavet and Oust – glittering remnants of the much-eroded Massif Amoricain mountain range.

These early peoples were followed by the Celts, including the tribe of the Redones (in the central area), the Coriosolites (on the northern coast) and the Veneti (in the south). The Celts owed their success to a high degree of adaptability and a shared language, which still exists today in a modified form as Breton. It is similar in grammar, vocabulary and syntax to Welsh and Gaelic. Like the monument builders who preceded them, the Celtic Gauls in Brittany worshipped nature, were skilled at working bronze, iron and wood and exceptionally adept at decorative art in precious metals and semi-precious stone. Many such pieces have survived as grave goods. The Celtic culture lasted for perhaps 2,000 years both in France and Britain and throughout other parts of Western Europe – even into what we now call the Balkans. But a little over 2,000 years ago a collection of warring tribes in Italy coalesced to form a nation state based on the nine hills of Rome. They copied some of the social structures and style of government of ancient Greece and were to become the most aggressively expansionist people in ancient times, with one of the largest and most enduring empires the world has ever seen.

The organised soldiery of Rome soon overcame even the superb horsemanship and bravery of the Celtic warriors and by 50 BC the whole of Europe from France to the Danube was administered by Rome – a condition that subsisted for nearly 500 years until the Roman Empire imploded under pressure from border warfare and a schism that threw Roman against Roman. When the legions marched away from Brittany in the fourth century, the Gallo-Romans that remained were assimilated into a fiercely independent, self-governing territory within France, but more deeply allied to Britain by trade and by blood.

The period of history between the fall of the Roman Empire and the rise of the petty Kingdoms and the Church is known as the Dark Ages – and there are very few written records to enlighten us about that time. From the little that we do know it seems there was a power vacuum and constant warfare as invaders swept down from the north and internal strife turned the productive Gallo-Roman countryside into a forested wilderness interspersed with fortified farmsteads. The Norsemen from Scandinavia, with their nautical traditions and warlike culture, settled along the coastal fringe of Brittany and adjoining Normandy. Gradually their influence came to be felt throughout the entire region since the Dukes of Normandy controlled the coast and the trade routes. A state of conflict existed, even after William of Normandy had conquered Britain, as the French and English kings fought for supremacy over the whole of the French mainland. To begin with the conflict which historians called the Hundred Years' War badly affected Brittany. The Bretons, with their affinity with nearby Britain, found themselves between the hammer and the anvil of opposing forces.

However, these resourceful people began to make good use of the many safe harbours around the rocky coast with a healthy trade in smuggling. Privateers were able to operate with impunity even while the two nations were at war – up to and throughout the Napoleonic Wars. During the Second World War members of the Resistance used the isolated coves and bays as a valuable conduit to help the Allies in their liberation of Europe.

Despite the essentially maritime traditions of the fiercely independent population, Brittany possesses two faces. Best known to tourists is the deeply indented coastline, the 'Armor' (the land by the sea.) Wherever you are the sea is never more than 60 miles away and once there were over a hundred sea driven mills around the coast. In the north-west of the region the Baie du Mont St Michel is sheltered from the worst winds by the Cotentin Peninsula and stretches to the world famous oyster beds at Cancale. Because the sea is trapped by the Peninsula the currents swirl around carrying nutrients and laying down productive mudflats and saltings which, in turn,

Pré Salé *sheep, Mont St. Michel*

attract immense flocks of waders and wildfowl, particularly
Brent geese. The saltings also provide good pastureland for the
renowned salt-flavoured lamb.

From St Malo, westwards, past Dinard and the river Rance
and on towards the huge oblong-shaped Baie de la Frênaye
and the incredible cliffs at Cap Fréhel the coastline is known
as the Côte d'Emeraude. It is littered with an abundance of
highly recommended beaches and convenient wildlife watching
points. A hydro-electric barrage has been built at the entrance
to the estuary of the river Rance. Half a mile long, it provides
power to a unique electricity generating station by means of the
force of the incoming and outgoing tides. The estuary itself,
which stretches inland as far as the ancient walled town of
Dinan, with its wealth of 15th- and 16th-century architecture,
provides some good general birdwatching areas.

Further west a cluster of granite islets and shoals (Ile de
Bréhat) have claimed many lives and ships over several thousands of years. Deeply indented estuaries with names like
Tréguier are reminiscent of Cornwall. They are the remains of
flooded valleys that silted up when the sea level rose after the

last Ice Age. This is the Côte de Granite Rose (The Pink Rock Coast) although it does require a certain stretch of the imagination, for the iron that stains the granite can range in colour from a deep rusty pink to blood red. Nonetheless the way in which these ancient rocks have reacted to time and weather has created an amazing landscape. It is also a fantastic area for seabird nest sites. Five kilometres out to sea, off the Pointe du Squéouel, lie Les Sept Iles – a scatter of tiny islets that constitute one of the finest seabird sanctuaries in the Channel.

Finistère – literally 'the end of the earth'– is a wild coastline of coves, wave-lashed beaches and yet more small islands – where grey seals haul out to breed in early autumn. Legend has attributed these rocks to a playful game of pétanque between the gentle giant Hok-Bas and the aggressive Gargantua. But, on dark stormy nights, it is the location of these razor-sharp rocks rather than their mythical origins that has concentrated the minds of generations of seafarers. The port of Roscoff is sheltered from the worst of the weather from the west and the north by the Ile de Batz and, though the entrance to the port itself is almost surrounded by submerged rocks, it was a base for privateers during the 16th and 17th centuries and almost certainly was an important area for the local people long before that – as is clearly shown by the massive Tumulus Barnenez (the burial place of an ancient chieftain), which looks out over the Baie de Morlaix and the Channel.

Around the Brest Peninsula, the constant, often violent, struggle between the Atlantic Ocean and the waters of the Western Approaches has shaped the coastline (known as the Côte de Légendes) into a maze of bays and inlets guarded by teeth of granite and ancient schists. The inlets in this part of Brittany are called Les Arbres, similar to the Welsh 'Aber' meaning river entrance. Just off the southern tip of the Brest Peninsula, and part of the Parc Régional d'Armorique, another small group of islands, dominated by the Ile Molène and Ile d'Ouessant, constitute a vital and well-known migration stop-over point for birds from the whole of the northern hemisphere, including the USA. The large tidal range created by the immense, almost landlocked, naturally flooded valley system that is the Rade de Brest provides tremendous feeding potential for the thousands of waders and wildfowl that winter here.

Coming into southern Brittany, past the Cap de la Chèvre and into the Baie de Douarnenez, the parallel between Brittany and the west of England is taken to an extraordinary degree in that this is the Côte de Cornouaille. In the days of ships powered by oar and by sail the Bay offered safe anchorage – indeed during the Hundred Years' War the French King, Louis XI, moored his fleet of galleys here. It's a lovely coast with long stretches of golden sand and charming resorts such as Bénodet, which sits at the entrance to the beautiful estuary of the river Odet – reaching 15 kilometres inland to Quimper, once the capital of King Gradlon (first King of Cornouaille).

Then there is the Archipel des Glénan – a multitude of islets with a few low sandy islands surrounded by clear water full of small fish that provide food for the terns and shags that nest here. One of the islands, St Nicholas, is a nature reserve, especially designated to protect one particular flower species, the Glénan daffodil.

Menhir

The whole of Brittany is renowned for dolmen, tumuli and menhirs. But the most incredible evidence of the administrative abilities and civil engineering skills of the

Carnac, Morbihan: The standing stones of Carnac march like
a petrified army across more than 12 kilometres,
a monument to the Neolithic builders

mysterious, long dead culture responsible for these monuments can be seen at Carnac in the south of the department of Morbihan – a 4,000-year-old world heritage site where alignments of individual stones march across the landscape for almost 12 kilometres like a petrified army – the object of worship and of fear. Even in the recent past, up to the 18th century, many people still thought that these alignments were the work of superhuman beings, or even gods. The attitude of the established church was ambivalent and only the sheer scale of the monument and the value put on the stones by the local inhabitants prevented their destruction.

The number of islands, peninsulas and flooded valleys along the length of the Brittany coast shows the rise in sea level since the end of the last Ice Age. By far the largest island lying off the Brittany coast is Belle Ile en Mer, an ancient volcanic plateau cut by green valleys with small rivers and a coastline of pretty estuaries and fine sandy beaches. On the mainland, one of the larger peninsulas is Presqu'île de Quiberon with its fashionable resort, sandbanks and beaches on the leeward side and caves, coves, cliffs and jagged rocks on the west coast facing the Atlantic Ocean. And then there is the Golfe du Morbihan, an immense flooded valley and, arguably, one of the most exciting wildlife sites in the whole of north-west France as well as the setting for a decisive sea battle when the Romans finally subdued the Veneti tribes of Gaul.

This then is the coast. But the other face of Brittany, the *Argoat* (pronounced argwat), is equally fascinating. Centuries-old farm tracks etched into the countryside have created a network of sunken lanes, edged on either side by low stone walls, or thick hedgerows where linnets, nightingales and warblers orchestrate their spring breeding season. In France, this type of countryside is known as *le Bocage* – and charming little villages with stone and half-timbered houses shelter in wooded valleys where the apple is king and the pear queen of the crop and raw material for a host of culinary and alcoholic delights.

For two million years the abrasive power of the European ice sheet reshaped the hard rocks of central Brittany. As the ice relaxed its grip, the land emerged clothed in fine acid sand, a remnant of the mountain ranges that had once run across the region. Eighteen thousand years of wind, sun and rain added some fertility, creating a mixture of sandy acidic upland soils that lie in bands over the ancient granite rock. These soils supported heathland where pines and birches and stunted oaks formed a broken canopy, while an extensive temperate 'rain forest' of oak, birch, ash and beech clothed the valleys.

Around about 5,000 years ago humankind began to clear the forest cover by fire and grazing. Winter rainfall, carried on the Atlantic winds, washed the nutrients and minerals down into the subsoil creating an iron-rich pan called 'podsol', locking in the nutrients needed by many plants – excepting heathers, heath and gorse (a legume that harbours nitrogen-fixing bacteria in its roots thereby creating its own food supply in a poor environment). These dry inland heaths provided excellent open, relatively tree-less grassland grazing for a pastoral society whose wealth was measured in flocks of sheep and fine horses. Known as 'Landes' after the Celtic word *lann* meaning gorse, they were often the focus for Celtic settlements. About half of inland Brittany was once acid heath. Most of it gone under the plough or conifer plantations. However, some fine examples still survive – the Landes de Lanvaux in Morbihan is the largest remnant, but heathland with its own special wildlife communities can be found in the Parc Natural d'Armorique, particularly near Huelgoat and in the Côtes d'Armor in the Landes de Liscuis.

More sophisticated methods of farming and the expectation and requirements of a burgeoning society brought about a gradual change in the management of the land. Farming was concentrated in the more fertile valley bottoms, leaving the hillsides to the trees and the wildlife. Nature has miraculous powers of recovery and the forests regenerated to cover areas that

Landes

Wild Thyme (Thymus serpyllum)*: The larval food plant of the large blue butterfly, often found growing on old ant hills and on south-facing cliff tops along many stretches of Brittany's coastline*

had formerly been pasture and in so doing provided a constant supply of natural food, not to mention timber for firewood and for building. The people began to discover and understand the importance of managing woodland for their own use, not only firewood and building, but coppice for staves, poles, handles for tools, pales, barrels and so on. For centuries this style of agriculture continued – until the Romans appeared on the scene with their more industrial style of agriculture and highly organised building projects, which used a huge amount of wood.

Down the centuries the forests have been managed and cut for a variety of purposes. Great swathes were felled to prop up the trenches in the First World War. Nevertheless Brittany is a still a well-wooded region, despite the terrible gales at the end of 1999. In the department of Morbihan the Forêt de Lanvaux consists of nearly 1,000 acres of trees ranging from conifers to beech, all entirely accessible to the public, and supports roe

Smooth newt (Triturus vulgaris): *A common newt found in ponds and slow-flowing streams all over Brittany including the old hammer ponds in the forest of Brocéliande, which are ideal for amphibians*

deer, boar and a host of small mammals including red squirrels and beech martens. The Couesnon Valley, in the department of Ille et Vilaine, is fed by acid streams and a mainly conifer forest sits on granite to the north and schist to the south, providing an ideal habitat for a host of wildlife adapted to live in conifer woodland. Red squirrels and pine martens are relatively common here. At the foot of the southern slopes of the chain of hills known as Monts d'Arrée lie several forested areas separated by deep valleys, many full of moss-covered granite boulders.

And then there is the Pays de Brocéliande. A wild forest in the valley of the river Aff, a place of magic and legend, it covers 7,000 hectares of land; much of it is in private hands, but laced through with a large number of footpaths. The wildlife here includes deer, wild boar and a variety of woodpeckers.

The Argoat is a land of rivers and canals as well as forests. Of the waterways in Brittany the Nantes–Brest Canal is probably the most important, crossing the departments of Loire Atlantique and Morbihan, linking up with the rivers Erdre and Oust and joining the Vilaine at the river port of Redon. Then it follows the river Blavet and runs into the river Aulne, which flows into the Rade de Brest. And the river Vilaine is probably one of the most beautiful, wending its way through lovely countryside and out into the Atlantic near La Roche Bernard.

Until fairly recently Brittany was remote from the rest of France. However, the rapid development of the transport system has meant that the regional capital, Rennes, is now only two hours from Paris by rail (TGV) and three hours by motor-way. Founded by the Celtic tribe of the Redones more than 2,000 years ago, Rennes became the capital of the Duchy of Brittany in the 11th century, and boasts some fine museums, art galleries and theatres. Of the other historic towns, St Malo, Lannion, Morlaix, Brest, Quimper, Concarneau and Vannes are all steeped in Breton traditions, with castles and museums aplenty. The old border towns of Châteaubriant and Fougères too have much to offer. Brest, France's most important naval base since the 17th century was completely destroyed during World War II, as was Lorient (also a naval base). Both have been rebuilt.

Brittany has long been a natural destination for Britons. Indeed, the name Brittany means Little Britain and came about in the third and fourth centuries as a result of a fusion of the Celtic immigrants driven from their homes across the Channel by Frankish invaders from Germany and the Low Countries and the Celtic inhabitants of north-western France. Today, in the 21st century, the flow of visitors across the Channel is vol-untary – driven by a desire to see and to enjoy this lovely land, the spectacular coastline, superb seafood and the cider that is a Breton speciality. Perhaps it is a race memory shared with the Bretons – this mutual love of a wild and beautiful environment shaped by nature and by humankind over the past 5,000 years.

Côtes d'Armor

Montagu's harrier

Introduction

Flanked on either side by the departments of Ille et Vilaine to the east and Finistère to the west, with Morbihan to the south, the considerable coastline of Côtes d'Armor stretches from Briac sur Mer, just west of Dinard, to Plestin les Grèves, several kilometres west of Lannion. It encompasses the Emerald Coast and the Pink Granite Coast where the granites and glittering mica-faceted schists are stained red with iron and worn into fantastic shapes by wind and sand and the action of the sea.

Ten thousand years ago, before the creation of the English Channel isolated Britain from its European neighbours, the hard rocks of this part of Brittany formed the high ground overlooking a heavily wooded landscape populated by herds of wild game – mammoth and aurochs, woolly rhino and herds of deer of three or four species, (one of which, the giant fallow deer, sported palmate antlers two metres across). When the land bridge between Britain and Europe was breached, the in-rushing seas began the ongoing development of a rugged coastline, the power of wind and waves sculpting the red stack cliffs like those at Cap Fréhel falling a hundred metres to the sea and isolating bird-rich islands like Les Sept Iles (now a nature reserve). The sea filled river valleys and created myriad bays – the small Baie de la Frênaye and the enormous Baie de Saint-Brieuc are two

Côte de Granite Rose

Thrift (Armeria maritime)*: The drifts of pink thrift grow in sunny maritime conditions, often along cliff tops*

excellent examples.

Along this new coastal fringe, what had once been wood-land was replaced within a few hundred years by salt marsh and cliffs and the beginnings of maritime heath. The change in land-scape brought about a decline in the herds of large mammals and the people began to manage the land in a different way, which is reflected in the landscape we see today.

The unexploited soils were enormously productive, both of simple crops of cereals and roots and native wild plants amenable to cultivation such as the wild cabbage, which still grows on the shifting sand peninsula at Sable d'Or and at Cap

Fréhel. This productivity allowed the highly organised pre-Celtic peoples to use some of their time to erect huge funerary monuments and build alignments of shaped or natural rocks to honour their deities or important individuals. The pastoral Celtic tribes that followed them brought sheep and cattle and the fine horses and hunting dogs that feature on their pottery, jewellery and ornaments. The Bronze Age was a time of prosperity and creativity: beautifully worked jewellery in gold, silver and bronze inset with semi-precious stones, and bronze weapons, have been recovered from tombs and votive sites, particularly in lakes and springs. These people, members of the tribes of the Veneti, the maritime Celts of the West Atlantic coast, were traders too with a remarkable mastery of the sea and what must have been superb navigational skills. Traffic across the Channel thrived.

The Romans, expanding their Empire, came to harness this prosperity and the Celts were no match for the regimented might of Rome. Hill forts were slighted and valley homesteads incorporated into organised estates. Surplus food was taken for the Roman army and revenue for Rome itself. Within a generation the Celtic inhabitants had been assimilated into the Roman way of doing things – a state of affairs that continued until the end of the fifth century AD when the Roman Empire collapsed and Germanic tribes from Eastern Europe rushed in to fill the power vacuum.

Since then the region and its people, as throughout most of France, has had to contend with many conflicts, including the Hundred Years' War, the French Revolution and two world wars. These days, it is much quieter (in the nicest possible way) and happy to be so. Tourism, forestry, agriculture, fishing and the cultivation of shellfish are predominant.

As far as tourism is concerned, there are many excellent resorts. The long stretch of beaches from Cap Fréhel to Cap d'Erquy are quite lovely, with trees coming right down to the sands in many cases. The two Caps themselves boast spectacular views. One of the most popular resorts along the Côte de Granite Rose is Tréguier, sitting on a hill above the estuary of the river Jaudy where yachts and cargo ships find shelter. Two gateway towers are the only remnants of past fortifications, but the town has an extremely fine cathedral, built of course from pink granite. Perros Guirec is probably the largest resort, typically well managed with plenty of facilities, including attractive clean beaches. It's also the jumping off point for day-trips to Les Sept Iles where otters and seals fish just off shore and the seals haul onto the rocks to breed. It can be a danger-ous coast for the unwary.

Standing at the entrance to the Léguer estuary is Lannion, the second largest town in the Côtes d'Armor. The high tidal range in this estuary allowed ships with deep drafts to unload at the old port and so encouraged trading, which is one of the reasons why it became the administrative capital of the depart-ment. Probably the largest town is Guingamp. Once a Roman way station, the old centre (worth a visit), is now surrounded by modern industry. However, it is still an agricultural centre and has an excellent market.

Geologically the countryside has much in common with Cornwall. The lovely flooded valley estuaries in both regions were created when the sea rose after the last Ice Age; the best examples in Côtes d'Armor are in the rivers Trieux, La Penze and the Léguer, which comes to the sea at Lannion carrying the rain from the high ground of the Monts d'Arrée down to the sea. From Belle Ile en Terre to Lannion the river Léguer runs through a heavily wooded valley of oak and beech – ancient woodland with ramsons and dog's mercury. Otters thrive here and the river is renowned for salmon and trout.

Inland, high open heaths, remnants of an eroded mountain range, support specialised heathland plants. Heath spotted orchids can be as common as bluebells in an English wood when the right conditions of moisture and sunshine combine on south facing hillsides. The rare sand lizard is found here. Dartford warblers breed in the gorse and heather, Montagu's harrier breed both on the heathland and on surrounding farmland. And as night falls the nightjars churr over the wild open heath, while little owls make their plaintive call from the bordering pine woodland.

Heath spotted orchid
(Dactylorhiza maculata)*:
Growing on acid soils on the wild
open territory of the heathlands*

It's a lovely land much influenced by the sea. Even in the deepest inland valleys the mist can roll in from the English Channel to blanket the hillsides, turning a woodland full of wildlife into a place of mystery with muffled sounds of running water and birdsong. The sea has always been of importance. Indeed the name of this region, Côtes d'Armor, is indicative of this historic importance – the word 'Armor' being Celtic for 'the sea' or 'of the sea'.

Wildlife

Baie de Beaussais

Just a few kilometres south-west of St Malo and Dinard is Ploubalay. Leave the town by the D786 heading west towards Matignon. Almost immediately you will find yourself along-side the Baie de Beaussais. There are several places to stop by the side of the road and an 'Aire' (designated parking and pic-nic area) where you can leave the car and explore on foot. The Grande Randonnée no. 34 runs almost the entire length of the bay and provides many excellent vantage points for watching the wildlife.

Evidence of a long association with humankind is seen in the salt marsh polders, areas of enclosed land that have been reclaimed from the sea. Large dollops of grass stand on columns of mud on the landward edge of the bay. These unusual-looking formations are caused by the sea, which erodes soft mud not consolidated by the roots of thrift and rice grass. Much of the thrift here has white flowers, which may be a genetic aberration, or a reaction to a mineral deficiency.

Look at Ploubalay on the map and it's easy to see why this area was reclaimed from the sea during the 17th and 18th centuries. Walls and dykes were built to enclose the mudflats and sea grass to create fertile grazing and good farmland. But

Baie de Beaussais: Thrift-covered mounds dot the extensive salt marsh of this wildlife-rich bay

the salt marsh has now recolonised much of the polderland and it has once again become a coastal wetland. These marvellous wildlife-rich mudflats are unusual in that they support sea-rush, rice grass and sea purslane, plants rare in Brittany; they also provide a vital stopover point for migratory birds from northern Europe, including dunlin, grey and golden plover, ruff and redshank. In winter through to early spring, Brent geese and small waders like ringed-plover rest and feed both here and in the estuary of the river Arguenon, just the other side of a small peninsula, where little egrets and the occasional flock of wintering avocets may be seen. As the winter migrants move north, their place is taken by a host of passage migrants, and the curlew that have fed on the worms and shellfish that abound in the mud are joined by whimbrels on their way to breeding territories in the high arctic tundra.

In spring the bay takes on a different style. At high tide parties of shelduck come onto the polders and on the land behind the dykes to rest and preen and split into pairs to lay eggs and hatch their brilliantly-coloured black and yellow ducklings in some of the many rabbit burrows perforating the banks and dykes around Ploubalay and also Lancieux (a little further along the coast going back towards Dinard).

Large numbers of warblers and other spring migrants like swallows and house martins gather on the coastal fringes prior to crossing the Channel to breed in the British Isles. And during late spring and early summer, the marshes are carpeted with flowers typical of salt laden soil – sea lavender, sea pinks, cushions of thrift and the deep green marsh samphire. So many plants means an abundance of butterflies with marsh fritillaries and European swallowtail butterflies taking advantage of the sunshine.

Where there are pools of standing fresh water, such as rain-filled puddles, marsh and edible frogs, and some common frogs, thrive. The unwary are harvested by grey herons and the little egrets that breed some distance from the bay, but use the fish and frog-rich margins as a valuable food source for their young.

Later in the year, the flow of bird migration moves in a southerly direction and peaks between August and October with large numbers of immature birds heading south, pausing only for a short time to rest and feed in the bushes and trees backing the bay, or on the food-rich mud that fills the gullies between the cushions of thrift.

Conditions here are dictated by the sea. One brilliantly sunny day might be followed by a grey damp blanket of sea mist. Nevertheless, it is this constant change of weather conditions that has helped to produce such a wonderful area with such a wide variety of wildlife and wildlife habitats.

It's a popular site with local schools and information about field visits can be obtained from the Association des Amis des Polders et Chemins Creux de Ploubalay, tel: 02 96 27 20 27.

Shelduck (Tadorna tadorna)*: A bird of salt marsh and estuary. Nests in disused rabbit burrows*

Samphire (Crithmum maritimum)*: Coastal salt marsh – often grown as a crop in disused salt pans*

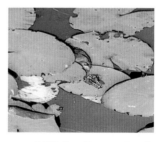

Edible frog (Rana esculenta)*: Much reduced in numbers through over collecting for the table. Close relative of the pool frog*

Cap Fréhel

Travel westwards along the coast from St Malo, over the barrage at the estuary of the river Rance and pick up the D168 to Ploubalay, then the D786 through Matignon to Fréhel. From Fréhel the D34 takes you along the scenic coast road right to the Cap where the nerve-tingling cliffs are stacked like a giant jumble

Lesser black-backed gull (Larus fuscus): *A large predatory gull of open sea. Nests along the coast, particularly on cliffs and islands*

of dark terracotta tiles. The layered red rock, coloured by mineral deposits, particularly iron-oxide, is whitewashed with guano from hundreds of nesting shags and kittiwakes and a few pairs of guillemots and razorbills. Indeed most of this Channel coast is seabird country. The more than adequate fishing in the shallow coastal waters encourages huge numbers and species of seabirds, particularly gannets, auks and kittiwakes.

The cliffs of Cap Fréhel reach nearly 100 metres high and are composed of sandstone, limestone and schist, but the softer strata have worn away over time leaving stacks, cut off from the main cliffs, and rising from the sea like natural skyscrapers. Their seeming fragility belies their strength and several promontories that jut out from the headland have so far resisted the power of the sea. However, in time, they too will be eroded and become isolated from the mainland, creating a multitude of new breeding ledges for the seabirds.

The birds have their favoured nesting places. The stacks and main cliffs are colonised by lesser black-backed gulls, which

Cap Fréhel: Stacks of rock strata that have eroded into perfect seabird nesting sites

Cap Fréhel – Banks of thrift along the cliff top

nest on the thrift-covered tops. A few greater black-backed gulls nest on grassy ledges strategically placed along the stacks and cliffs – as well as being fish-eaters they are also egg thieves and opportunist predators. Their sheer size and the volume of food they need to consume during the breeding season restricts their numbers in relation to their lesser black-backed cousins. A substantial colony of herring gulls takes advantage of cracks and gullies in the rocks to build their scrappy nests; they depend for food on the fishing fleets that ply the Channel. Above the auk colonies, a few pairs of fulmars breed on ledges. They are a success story. Until the beginning of the 20th century and a more industrialised method of fishing, fulmars as a species were confined to the Hebridean Islands and the far north. Now they capitalise on the waste products thrown over-board from trawlers and from drift net fishing boats and have spread down the British coast and crossed the Channel in the last quarter of the 20th century.

The black-backed gulls (both greater and lesser species) cause a constant state of alarm in the kittiwake colony, and the success of these gulls may also be linked to a reduction in the number of auks. In fact, both kittiwakes and auks are declining, and the reasons, though not yet clearly understood, may be linked to oil pollution in their wintering sites.

The wind off the sea creates turbulent updraughts in which ravens play, although they prefer to nest further along the cliffs away from the main colonies of gulls, auks and human inter-ference. A small, but healthy population of rock doves, which would appear to be a genuinely wild population relatively untainted by genes from domestic pigeons, are prey to the increasing numbers of peregrine falcons that winter along this dramatic coastline. The natural crevices are also home to stock doves, another reason for the peregrines' recolonisation of these cliffs. As yet these superb falcons are winter visitors only, with immature birds predominating, but with an increasing breeding population along the Channel coast of the British Isles it can be only a matter of time before they attempt to nest here. Cap Fréhel was once a noted peregrine breeding eyrie, but the use of persistent pesticides and persecution by game interests brought the peregrine populations over the whole of Europe to a low ebb. Fortunately, they are now recovering and every year their numbers increase.

Smaller birds are much in evidence too, with a healthy breeding population of black redstarts at the top of the cliffs with whinchats, stonechats and wheatears in the scrub that thrives on the cliff top heathland. The melodious warbler breeds here, a rare occurrence for Brittany, but it's not easy to see and can confused with the Icterine warbler. The head of the former is rounded with more yellow above the eye and on the breast. The back and tail are evenly coloured olive and as the name suggests, the song is melodic and extended with no jar-ring or harsh notes. The head of the Icterine warbler is more triangular, sloping strongly from the base of the bill to the back of the head. The back and tail are pale olive in colour, the wing feathers clearly defined and the song resembles that of a marsh warbler with a mixture of harsh and melodic notes.

The heathland along the top of the cliffs is home to a size-able population of early purple orchids and heath spotted orchids. Further back from the edge of the cliffs deep gullies shelter small copses of goat willow and gorse from the full force of the Channel gales. These little clumps of vegetation harbour large numbers of moths and butterfly species, including a small population of heath fritillary butterflies. Map butterflies, small tortoise-shell and peacock butterflies take advantage of areas of net-tle that grow in the fertile ground in the lee of the trees and bushes. These small copses also provide an area where sea buckthorn can get a toe-hold, much to the delight of brim-stone butterflies for which this plant is an alternative food source.

Early purple orchid (Orchis mascula): *Grows along woodland rides in company with stichwort and bluebells. Once thought to be an aphrodisiac because of the double tubers, but this has no basis in fact. It also thrives in the forests at Brocéliande*

Cap Fréhel, by its very nature, is a site of constant interest and fascination. The prox-imity of the Channel with its ever-changing weather conditions creates a variety of micro-climates. Brilliant spring sunshine might be bathing the heathland and bringing the birds into song while a few hundred metres away the cliff face is clothed in dense mist rolling in off the Channel. Such a contrast creates a unique mixture of maritime heath and dramatic coastline that

Small tortoiseshell butterfly (Aglais urticae) *on Sedum. A common butterfly of woodland margins and gardens. Lays eggs on nettle*

Peacock butterfly (Inachis io): *A nettle-feeding butterfly, arguably the most beautiful of the European insects*

makes this protected French nature reserve a site that should not be missed.

Guided walks are organised during spring and summer, starting from the imposing lighthouse, which warns mariners to stay away from this dangerous coastline.

Rance Estuary

Leave St Malo, head westwards towards Dinard and pick up the D168, which takes you across the barrage (the tidal power station) at the seaward end of the river Rance. In common with many estuaries this one comes into its own during autumn through to late winter with an influx of waders from all over northern Europe and the British Isles. The sky can be literally full of waders, put up by birds of prey like osprey, black kite, merlin and immature peregrine falcons that use this estuary as a migration stopover point.

At the entrance to the estuary the entire area is criss-crossed with a filigree of gullies and channels, which allows the sea to freshen and reinvigorate the marsh on a twice daily basis. In summer, the high tide line provides ample feeding for small birds like goldfinches and meadow pipits as they search the tide line spoil for seeds and insects. Between the shoreline and the

Rance Estuary, Côtes d'Armor: Once a refuge for the corsairs and privateers who harried English merchant shipping in the Channel

Mixed wader flocks: Grey plover (Pluvialis squatarola), *redshank* (Tringa tetanus), *and knot* (Calidris canutus)

coastal road a large number of salt-marsh-adapted flowering plants like thrift and sea lavender thrive and the tallest thistles are quickly taken over by male stonechats as song posts. Skylarks breed in the dry fringes of land behind the saltings and are among the specialities here, together with the yellow wagtails (usually the British subspecies, recognised by the brighter yellow colouring.) The continental subspecies (blue-headed wagtail) also occurs here and both species of these pretty and active summer migrants nest in the tufts of salt marsh (although it can be difficult to distinguish between the two in the field).

The creation of the barrage has altered the tidal pattern so that now the mud flats on the lower estuary remain partially submerged whatever the state of the tide. This creates ideal conditions for wintering duck and parties of Brent geese. Shelduck, always a feature of estuaries and salt marsh, are common on the Rance and the salt marsh acts as a magnet for flocks of widgeon and pintail. The spring and summer influx of birds is most marked by the presence of common and Arctic terns. The former stay for the summer and catch small fry in the fish-rich waters.

The river Rance is navigable as far inland as the ancient town of Dinan, and day-tripper boats run excursions from the

Barrage to Dinan and back again. From the boat you might see the terns fishing and the occasional guillemot picking off shrimps in the swirls and eddies. In civilised French fashion these tripper boats will provide lunch as an optional extra, or even arrange an evening excursion with dinner. Although there's an enormous amount of wildlife on the river at night its presence will be heard rather than seen – mostly duck and hooting owls.

Les Sept Isles

Approximately half way along the Channel coast of Brittany, a few kilometres north of Lannion on the D788, is the popular holiday resort of Perros Guirec with its sandy beaches, busy marina, casino and hydrotherapy centre. Its position on the lovely Côte de Granite Rose makes it an ideal base for exploring the local countryside. But from a wildlife point of view, especially seabirds, it is the scatter of granite islands and islets five kilometres off the coast that is the main attraction here.

In the period of time, 50 million or so years ago, which constituted the European and northern Asian mountain-building phase in the earth's history, cracks and fissures along the edge of the tectonic plates leaked mineral-rich granite in between layers of sedimentary rock. Intervening aeons of weather and water erosion carved away the softer rock leaving behind pillars, stacks and cliffs of granite that gradually oxidised, creating the colours and textures of the Côte de Granite Rose and the shape of the Sept Iles archipelago. The Atlantic Ocean rushed in to fill the Channel a number of times during this period of millions of years, and the power of the sea, and the rocks and sand carried along with it, eroded the loose granite to create these islands; a process that continues to this day.

A noted wildlife site since 1912 and designated a nature reserve in 1976, the islands constitute the most important nesting site for seabirds in the whole of France. Thirteen species of birds nest here with probably 12,000 birds at the height of the breeding season, including gannet, razorbill, black guillemot, kittiwake, herring gull, greater and lesser black-backed gulls, fulmar, raven, rock pipit, wheatear and the occasional peregrine falcon.

This is also the only place in the whole of France where puffins nest. These fascinating little birds spend most of their life far out to sea where they feed on surface shoaling fish like sprats and sand eels. In early spring they come together in great gatherings called rafts to form pairs (often the pairs will have bred together the previous year). Both males and females develop the parrot-like coloured bill sheath that is part of the breeding plumage and which appears to have no particular function other than a form of decoration to attract a member of the opposite sex. Tiny birds, no bigger than a town pigeon, they leave the water and gather on shore like a small army of troops, parading pompously up and down the thrifty turf. Eventually the pairs seek out their nesting burrows in the cliff top turf

Côte de Granite Rose

where they lay a single egg and rear the chick in the dark confines of the burrow. The chick is fed on sand eels and the parents travel great distances on tiny whirring wings to fetch food for the young. The breeding season must be an enormous strain on birds with such a limited power of flight. The local gulls, particularly herring gulls and lesser black-backed gulls attack the home-coming puffins as they return to the burrows laden with fish, carried head to tail along the odd-looking beak. The gulls force the unfortunate puffins to drop their catch, which the gulls then pick up in flight. Despite this impediment the puffin colony manages to rear a reasonable number of chicks.

When night falls the puffins cease their labours, but Manx shearwaters, unrelated to the puffins but equally vulnerable to

Puffins (Fratercula artica): *These small clown-like birds adopt the well-known coloured bill and eye ornaments only in the breeding season. Seen off the Channel coast, they breed on Les Sept Iles, but are declining in numbers*

attack from the gulls, return, under the cover of darkness, to their chicks hidden away in a burrow. The sound of Manx shearwaters at night is eerie and has been likened to souls in torment; it may well have given rise to many of the myths and tales of mermaids and sea monsters around these islands.

Actually, Les Sept Iles includes more than the seven islands that give this extraordinary archipelago its name, but most of them are off limits to landing parties. However, boats run out from Trestraou beach to the Ile aux Moines and allow visitors ashore for an hour or two. It had been used by the British as a base to attack the French coast, and so a fort was built in the 18th century to prevent further raids. The view from this fort and the lighthouse, which warns of the dangers to shipping posed by these notorious rocks, is wonderful. With a telescope it's possible to see the common tern colonies on the Ile Plate. These beautiful seabirds plunge-dive for small fry in the waters between the islands. This particular island also supports nesting shelduck.

Although the day-tripper boats from Perros Guirec only stop at Ile aux Moines, they approach all the other most interesting islands in the group and allow a good view of the colonies along the cliffs. This is a spring and summer reserve, best when the birds are nesting, or gathering on the sea prior to nesting, or at the end of the summer when the young leave the nest and 'raft' before heading off to their winter quarters all over the northern hemisphere.

In early May the first puffins will be gathering on the sea, particularly around the Ile de Rousic, which also supports the largest seabird colony, including thousands of gannets. The smell of the gannets, especially down wind, is strong. Malban is home to large colonies of shags and cormorants and fulmar petrels, which are taking over more and more nesting ledges as their inevitable southward spread is consolidated along both sides of the Channel. The Ile de Bono supports large numbers of seabirds too and some ravens and it's well worth scanning the sky for birds of prey. The presence of large numbers of razorbills and guillemots in early spring is a feature of all of these extraordinary islands.

In spring the water between the mainland and the islands is particularly busy with birds, but you might also see occasional groups of grey seals. The creation of the nature reserve has given these animals a better level of protection. Traditionally regarded by fishermen as competitors for the available fish stocks, in former years the number of grey seals has been kept in check by shooting and by culling the pups. More recently these delightful creatures have begun to increase to perhaps something like the number that this archipelago might be expected to support naturally. The seals can be trusting and will bob about in the water quite close to the boat with a curious but short-sighted expression. They can be seen during most months of the year and breed in late autumn.

Smaller passerines are in evidence too. Wheatears nest in some of the disused puffin, petrel and shearwater burrows and rock pipits rear their chicks in crevices around the cliffs. The pressure of such large numbers of seabirds means that plant life is limited, but thrift and sea plantain thrive in spite of the birds and there is also sea campion, common sea lavender and a small amount of sea rocket.

Islands, by their very nature, create their own magic. These islands have history and wildlife in full measure. Seen on a sunny day in spring with the light falling on the dazzling white plumage of the birds in the gannet colony, it's easy to see why some ornithologists make a regular pilgrimage to this scatter of granite shards every year.

The LPO (Ligue pour la Protection des Oiseaux) organise trips on Saturdays throughout the summer, when they visit the bird observatory on Ile Grande.

Towns and Villages

Dinan

One of the best preserved medieval towns in Brittany, Dinan has excellent examples of timber-framed and arcaded buildings particularly along the rue de l'Horloge and rue de l'Apport with their collection of restaurants and cafés. The famous restaurant La Mere Pourcel sits in the Place des Merches in a fine 15th -century half-timbered building, and in between the rue de la Cordonnerie and rue du Petit Pain is the market and a lovely group of centuries-old little shops.

This delightful remnant of a past era owes its existence to the fact that it lies on the river Rance. The town sits some way inland from the estuary, but in medieval times the river trade, both further inland and out to sea brought enormous wealth to the town merchants. During the 18th century the import and export of wool and woolen cloth consolidated this prosperity.

The 14th-century castle is well worth a visit. Designed by the same man who built the Tour Solidor at St Malo it was, at one and the same time, a defensive fortress and a residence with a chapel. Today you can enjoy the museum housed in the keep. Part of the Bayeux Tapestry shows the siege of Dinan in 1065, just before William Duke of Normandy conquered England, and the museum provides a clear idea of how the town developed from a simple village into what it has become today.

The Basilica of St Sauveur is outstanding. A Crusader Knight vowed that if he returned from the Holy Wars he would build a church. Consequently St Sauveur's was influenced by Byzantine art, and its architecture is unparalleled in Brittany. In medieval times the church was enlarged, and it was designated a Basilica in the 1950s. Today, among many lovely religious treasures, it houses a 12th-century font, a 15th-century alabaster Virgin made in Nottingham, and splendid 17th- and 18th-century altarpieces.

From the Jerzual gate the rue du Petit Fort runs steeply downhill to the old port. This is the artists' quarter with quay-side cafés and restaurants and a glorious view of the town and of the marvellous 19th-century viaduct. A useful little tourist train saves walking back up to the town on its high vantage point.

Quintin

The rainfall in Brittany not only produces a general impression of verdant fertility, it creates an excellent climate for the growth and process of turning flax into linen thread. One of the oldest types of cloth made from vegetable fibres, specimens of flaxen cloth have been found in Iron Age peat bog burials in Denmark and Germany.

For thousands of years this practical durable material was spun and woven at the hearth, but as production from the nearby Payes de Léone increased in response to demand from the artisan weavers in the Quintin region, so the numbers of people who made their living from flax increased. By the beginning of the 18th century improvements in technique and finishing meant that 'Quintin' linen was famed for its quality across Europe. The fine linen thread produced by multitudes of spinsters was also the raw material for the intricate lace-work used to make the famous tall Breton head-dresses and cuffs and collars for the menfolk.

Prior to the revolution nearly a thousand people were employed in this trade, but by the time stability returned the labour intensive linen trade had been overtaken by the industrial production of linen in Britain, coupled with the growing popularity of King Cotton, a trade dominated by the British and Prussians. Nevertheless the town retains a flavour of its prosperity in the century leading up to the Revolution in 1789 in the old houses in the Grande Rue. These sturdy artisan dwellings tell of the time when the flaxen thread was the mainstay of the town's weavers. There is an architectural echo of a past age in the steeply raked streets and the old houses that still stand near the Place 1830 and in the workshops of a number of highly skilled artisans and artists in materials as diverse as stained glass and clocks, carved stone and furniture.

The Basilica of Notre Dame is dedicated to spinsters and in the past apprentice spinners would bring offerings of flax. The reliquary is reputed to hold a fragment of cloth from the Virgin's belt.

St Brieuc

A Welsh monk called Brieuc founded a religious order in the town of St Tréguier and, later in the ninth century, the seat of the bishop moved to the town that now bears his name. At that time it was only a small place, but it gradually became more prosperous and in 1790 was designated the administrative capital of the department. The Industrial Revolution, born in Britain, was slow to reach France and it was only after the railway came to this region in the late 19th century that expansion took place and the iron and steel works spread out into the surrounding countryside. This led to changes in architecture and town planning and also to the creation of a thriving modern art culture among the artist's colony here. However, signs of the old town can be found in the narrow streets and ornate, half-timbered buildings that surround the cathedral.

The cathedral, dedicated to St Etienne, has enjoyed a somewhat chequered history. An early ninth-century wooden building succumbed to fire and was followed by a stone church in the tenth century, which stood until the English burned it down during the 14th century. Another church rose from the ashes in the 1380s and remained for two hundred years before being pillaged and damaged by invaders. The anti-religious feelings aroused by the French Revolution led to the appropriation of many old churches for more secular purposes and the cathedral was used to manufacture ingredients for gunpowder. However, in spite of considerable damage to the interior woodwork, a certain amount of the original decoration remains, including a wooden altarpiece by Yves Corlay.

Moving away from the cathedral precincts, the rue de la Corderie has a fine example of art deco shell mosaic decorating the front of no. 20. The fan-shaped design was created by an Italian immigrant family, the Odoricos, who brought the art of mosaic with them from their homeland. Nos. 20 and 24 are quite startling with the latter decked out in a design executed in blue glass.

St Brieuc lies in the valley of the river Gouëdic and it's possible to walk the hills above the town and enjoy some impressive views.

Sables d'Or les Pins

'The most beautiful beach in Brittany.' It's not easy to justify such a claim but, undoubtedly, the beach here is lovely: a wide arc of golden sand backed by low cliffs and dunes and pine woods. The idea of using this gorgeous setting for a resort came from two entrepreneurs, Brouard and Launay, but their vision foundered in the 1929 stock market crash and many of the building plots, already cleared and levelled, reverted to nature. Nevertheless, it has grown into an elegant town, nestling quietly against a backdrop of trees looking out over its 'most beautiful beach.'

Tréguier

Built on a hill where the two arms of the river Jaudy meet and head towards the sea through a long, spectacular estuary, Tréguier was founded in the sixth century by a Welsh monk called St Tugdual or Tudwal and has been an important religious centre ever since.

The pink granite cathedral of St Tugdual, begun in the 12th century, has been added to over the centuries in a variety of styles from Gothic onwards. It has three entrance porches – Ladres, Cloches and Peuple, all of them heavily carved. As well as religion, the city's early years were marked by strong commercial activity in the wine trade and printing, as well as the port's trade in grain and wool. Many of the old wood-framed houses built by merchants and artisans on the strength of the prosperity created by trade still remain. The French Revolution and its aftermath dealt a grievous blow to this trade and the commercial centre never really recovered. However, it is now quietly prosperous with a thriving tourist industry, and very much worth visiting.

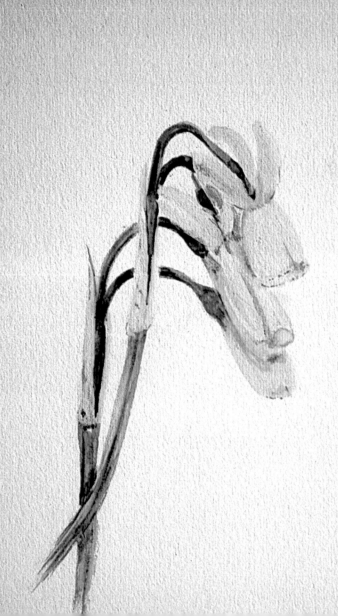

Finistère

Glenan daffodil

Introduction

Finistère means literally 'the end of the earth' and, as far as France is concerned, the Brest Peninsula with Finistère at its westernmost tip is indeed the end of the earth – thrusting out into the Atlantic like a lion's head with its mouth wide open in defiance of some of the roughest, most turbulent seas in Europe where two major currents meet in the Western Approaches to the English Channel.

With one of the longest coastlines of all the French departments, Finistère boasts miles of beaches of pale sand backed by dunes. One of the loveliest is the Anse des Blancs-Sablons, a protected natural site made up of two kilometres of white sand just to the north of Le Conquet. Situated at the mouth of a river on a rocky peninsula, behind the beach, the dunes rise to 30 metres.

Deep estuaries, broad reaches and quiet harbours provide an abundance of food and safe refuge for wildlife. The Grève de Goulven on the Channel coast between Plouescat and Brignogan-Plages is an enormous sheltered bay supporting migrant waders and sea duck. In between the beaches and holiday resorts, lie sheltered inlets and estuaries called Abers, the old Celtic word for an estuary (the same word as used in

Lesconil: Rocks sculpted by the wind

Welsh). The western Abers, as they are known, Aber Wrat'h, Aber Benoît and Aber Ildut, are sunken valleys full of silt and rich in wildlife. The granite that lines Aber Ildut, the southernmost of the three, was much exploited and used to build the Place de la Concorde in Paris.

It's an exciting coastline, littered with rocky islets and small islands marooned in the wild seas during winter gales, the wind and waves crashing onto the shore in a welter of flying spray after the 3,000 mile fetch from the American continent. But, in summer, these same islands are set like jewels in blue-green waters. Among the most important, from a wildlife point of view, are those that make up the Ushant archipelago, one of the remotest places in Brittany, which has played a vital role in research into bird migration. The wide expanse of the Rade de Brest is marvellous for wildlife too, with duck, geese and waders and rarities blown off course from North America. Further down the coast, the Pointe de Raz and Raz de Sein, classed as a 'Grand Site National', also attract birdwatchers.

If Finistère resembles a roaring lion, then the Crozon Peninsula must be the tongue. The whole peninsula is designated a regional park with some spectacular cliffs, particularly the caps on the western tip. In between are quiet beaches backed by reed-fringed meres where avocets, black-winged stilts and terns breed in quiet profusion.

Naturally, the region is not all coast and dunes. The whole area from the Ile d'Ouessant to the Forêt de Fréau far inland on the spine of the ancient eroded mountain chain of the Massif des Monts d'Arrée, is designated 'Le Parc Naturel Régional d'Armorique'. It is a paradise for wildlife with 172,000 hectares (approximately 600 square miles) of bocage, country lanes, fields, forests, deep wooded valleys and wild heaths where curlew call and the pale wings of Montagu's harriers ride the slightest breeze. When the European ice sheet melted, the water roared to the sea across this part of France extracting precious

Marshmallow (Althaea officinalis): *This tall stately plant grows on south-facing sand banks behind the dunes. The fleshy roots are the original source of the marshmallow 'sweet' and the sap from the roots is also used as a remedy for indigestion. Marshmallows need warmth and lime-rich sandy soil and grow in abundance in southern Finistère*

Bloody cranesbill (Geranium sanguineum): *Usually found growing on sand dunes all along Brittany's coast. The bright green foliage and brilliant purple-red flowers form huge cushions of colour in an otherwise seemingly sterile environment*

metals as it eroded the rock; and the effect of water is seen all across the region from the rain-scoured hills of the Landes (heathlands) to the wet mossy valley bogs and granite boulders that litter the valleys. The rivers have rounded these boulders and, in some places, jumbled them into giant heaps. The area around Huelgoat (pronounced Hell-gwat) where the rivers Squirrou and Aulne meet is reminiscent of Becky Falls on Dartmoor in the west of England with massive rocks and deep pools between tree-covered banks.

The river Aulne runs to the sea into the Rade de Brest through a twisting estuary and this almost enclosed sea is the destination for many other rivers too. The Elorn, Daulas and Faou all flow into the Rade and, together with the river Aulne, were once a rich source of gold and silver, which was panned, and for lead, the heavy metal mined by the Romans. The lead ore is exposed where the rivers cut down through the rock. In southern Brittany, the rivers Pont l'Abbé, Odet, Aven and Belon run directly into the Atlantic. Of the major towns,

Huelgoat: High above the old lead and silver workings,
the lake at Huelgoat provided water for crushing mills

Lichen on rocks growing at Lesconil

Quimper is the department's regional headquarters, a charming, prosperous place famous for its pottery. Douarnenez, tucked into one corner of the Baie de Douarnenez, is also a major fishing port and was once a centre for the production of *garum* (a popular fermented fish oil used by the Romans as a condiment.) On the other hand, Brest, founded by the Romans, developed into a strategic naval base, mainly because of the size and importance of the Rade de Brest: but this trick of fate restricted its use as a trading or fishing port and so limited its wealth.

Argoat is the Celtic Breton word for inland and Armor is the Celtic Breton for coast. Land and sea are intertwined like the endless knot design of an Iron Age jewel and the Celtic link between the Bretons and the people of western England and Wales goes back even beyond the mass immigration from Britain to north-western France in the chaos of the Dark Ages. For more than 2,000 years tin, gold, cider, fish, slaves and hunting dogs have been traded between the two seafaring nations.

The movement of modern humans across the landscape of

Quimper: A view towards the twin spires of the cathedral of St Corentin

post-Ice Age Europe brought about the replacement of the first hunter-gatherer peoples. They were followed by a more settled pastoral society with considerable cultural and religious strengths, almost certainly attracted to this region because of the easily panned gold, excellent grazing and high ground of the Monts d'Arrée as a fine place on which to erect their standing stones and stone-lined tombs and menhir.

Possibly because of its remoteness it was one of the last regions to be conquered by the Romans, and hence Armorica is the home base of Asterix the Gaul and his friend the menhir delivery man Obelix. To this day there is fierce pride in Breton independence and traditions, manifested in the popularity of

Celtic music with its thin tenor bagpipe notes and sharp drums, and robust songs that tell of love and battles and kinship.

The link between Britain and the Bretons of Finistère is immortalised in the story of Tristan and Iseult (Tristram and Isolde are the British names). Tristram, Prince of Leon in north Finistère was sent by his uncle King Mark of Cornouaille (Cornwall) to escort Iseult, the king's betrothed, from Ireland to Brittany. On the way they fell in love and, as with all good legends, their tragic story has been told down the ages by many poets and playwrights, culminating in Wagner's magnificent opera.

These days Finistère is one of the most successful regions in France, attracting visitors from all over the world to come and enjoy the dramatic coastal scenery and the quiet peacefulness of the inland valleys and heaths. The sea's influence is everywhere, including the wonderful dishes based on fish and shellfish and served in delicious cream and cider sauces. On market day, fresh seafood fills the air with mouth-watering smells. But for all the predominance of water, it is essentially a sunny region, alive with birdsong and the sounds of wild creatures, its unspoiled meadows full of butterflies.

Wildlife

Forêt Domaniale de Huelgoat

Returning to the D769 from the reserve at Cragou, the road runs south for about three kilometres and is joined at Berrien by the D14. Both roads lead to the town of Huelgoat. Encompassed in this sugar-loaf-shaped parcel of hilly land, cut deep with river valleys, are the Gouffre and Camp d'Artus, places connected to Arthurian legend.

Sitting as it does on the southern slopes of the Monts d'Arrée – an ancient mountain range eroded through time and the elements – the area around Huelgoat consists of dense woodland following a valley and river system that shows evidence of the great floods and upheavals that occurred as the European ice sheet receded. Water from the melting glaciers tumbled huge granite boulders, some as big as houses, to clog up the steep-sided valleys and bubbling streams with an artistically assembled sculpture of mossy mounds. With so much woodland and so many streams, the whole area is rich in wildlife.

The forest is part of a semi-continuous area of woodland that clothes the hillsides of this ancient landscape. Exploited by humankind for thousands of years, in the past these hills yielded great wealth. Lead mines were dug into the hard rock along the

Gouffre, Huelgoat

Gouffre, Huelgoat: The last Ice Age left behind a scatter of huge waterworn boulders clothed in thick green moss, creating a magical series of water-scapes

valley of the river Fao. There were other rare metals too, including silver; indeed the mines were so productive of this precious metal that part of the river to the east of Huelgoat came to be known as Argent, 'The Silver River'. The mines are worked out now, but the name remains as a reminder of past glories.

The river finds its way into a tree-fringed lake in the town of Huelgoat and out again alongside the D769 and through a maze of moss-covered, water-worn boulders, emerging in pools of reflective water, alive in spring and summer with dragonflies and damselflies. Several lay-bys allow you to stop and explore. In one direction steps lead down to the dramatic Gouffre, and in another take you up to a marvellous viewpoint, looking over the treetops down into the valley. The water in the pools is acid, but productive of caddis and sedges (roof-winged flies) that attract swallows, martins and swifts. Small trout grow portly on the abundant summer feeding, which is just as well for they will have to contend with the powerful flash floods that periodically thunder down the valley.

The deep, almost windless, boulder-strewn valleys have their own microclimate. Old trees, survivors of past gales, are full of nest sites and food potential for insects like stag beetles (the larvae feed on rotting wood) and hunting predatory ground beetles, which live on other beetles and soft-bodied insects. The beetles provide a livelihood for the little owls, which peer out from tree holes, looking like clockwork toys.

Such rugged landscape does not encourage agriculture; in consequence the land has been left to its natural woodland cover. The resulting mixture of oak, ash, Scots pine and chestnut is home to a wide range of forest birds and mammals. Wild boar feature here, though they are naturally shy of human contact. Red squirrels and pine martens are also present and, at the edge of town, or in and around farm buildings, the shy, nocturnal beech marten searches out birds, rats and mice. They will

Little owl

also take chickens, which makes them less than popular with farmers.

Forest bird life varies from the river valley to the high ground. The main predator in the wooded valleys is the sparrow-hawk because of its ability to twist and turn, chasing small birds through the trees. Above the forest, common buzzards, the largest birds of prey here, hunt squirrels in the canopy and rabbits in the clearings and rides. In early spring, pied flycatchers and redstarts depend on the oak trees for food and nest sites and fill the air with their lovely songs. As spring develops, woodcock, which have used the woodlands in winter as a feeding ground, establish territory and patrol a rectangle of forest at tree height on what is called the 'roding' flight. This is when the males patrol the territorial boundary making a strange sound resembling a grunting sneeze. The female scrapes out a nest on the ground. She sits so tight and is so superbly camouflaged that it's possible to walk right up to the nest without seeing it – and she will not leave her eggs until the very last moment.

The hurricane that swept across southern Britain in 1987 brought down many trees in this area too. But storm damage in a forest is not always detrimental, certainly not in the long term. The canopy is opened up. Light reaches right down to the woodland floor and, at Huelgoat, the result has been a burgeoning of wild flowers including primrose, greater stitchwort and oxlip – and an explosion of tree saplings. These provide a valuable food source in the form of caterpillars of a wide range of moth species – from the micro-Lepidoptera that fly around the sapling oaks, to large gaudy elephant hawk moths, the larvae of which feed on willow herb.

In this lovely forest, when the sunlight shafts down through the trees onto the moss-carpeted woodland floor and the birds are in full song, it's not hard to imagine King Arthur and his knights rescuing damsels in distress, or the old giants of legend, particularly Gargantua, who had a penchant for throwing rocks

Elephant hawk moth (Deilephila elpnor): *A large colourful moth, apparently a tropical species. The larval food plant is rosebay willow herb and the larva is large and grey and trunk-like – hence the name*

all over Brittany, hurling boulders down the hillside and into the valleys, just for the fun of it.

Cragou

About 20 kilometres south of Morlaix, the southern sector of the parish of Le Cloitre St Thégonnec, a beautiful yet unforgiving landscape, is populated with a scatter of tiny villages, the Celtic names Kergreis, Kergorre and Kerbrian indicating the length of time this region has been inhabited by humankind. Along the D769, just outside Penmergues, the D111, a pleasant country road, rises to meet the heathlands. Shown on the map as Rochers du Cragou, this substantial reserve (300 hectares

Cragou

under protection) is founded on sharp-edged rocks of red and green schist, which support a unique mix of heathland, relic broadleaved forest and agricultural land.

The whole of this region lies at the foothills of the Monts d'Arrée, the acid remnants of a long-eroded mountain chain pushed up by a mountain-building phase that creased and crumpled this part of France 50 million years ago. What were once towering peaks have long since been reduced to boulders and sand, ground by the elements and the mill of time, leaving behind no more than rolling hills. Nevertheless the landscape still holds a quiet echo of the majesty of the old mountain chain, though these days it is found in the deep boggy valleys that give birth to swift-flowing, boulder-filled rivers. The water is the colour of apple brandy and harbours dippers and golden-sided brown trout, both of which pursue the caddis larvae.

The ridges that dominate the area are topped with natural cairns of igneous rock that glitters with quartz, mica and a hint of silver and gold, and which degrades slowly into a naturally acid soil. On these ridges grow the remnants of a forest of stunted oaks, digging their strong roots deep into cracks in the rock to hold on to the sparse soil, whatever the wind may do. These trees provide shelter and nest sites for the migrant warblers and for carrion crows as well as the occasional common buzzard.

Large birds of prey, particularly harriers, are a feature here. Both Montagu's harrier and hen harrier breed either within the confines of the reserve, or on the surrounding farmland, and in spring, the display flight is marvellous to see with the males passing food to the females to cement the pair bond, appearing to defy gravity as they hang together in mid air.

Montagu's harriers quarter the bog and open heathland on pale wings held in a shallow V, in a seemingly effortless search for the small birds and mammals that form the bulk of their prey. The larger hen harrier hunts birds up to and including the

Cross-leaved heath (Erica detralix)*: A shrub of bogs and wet heathland. Often found with bell heather in spite of the different habitats required. Bell heather thrives on the dry tussocks while the cross-leaved heath nestles in wet hollows*

size of coot and moorhen. Both female Montagu's harrier and female hen harrier are brown above with a white rump patch and they are difficult to tell apart. It's easier to distinguish between the males, even without binoculars. Both have pale grey plumage with dark wing tips, but the wing tip of Montagu's harrier is shaded from grey to black with a black band tapering across the primaries to the elbow of the wing;.The hen harriers' sharply defined dark wing tip lacks this black band. They have only a dark grey margin to the trailing edge.

Other birds of prey include kestrels, hobby falcons, sparrow-hawks and common buzzard, and the occasional honey buzzard. The presence of so many species of raptors indicates the productivity of this fascinating area. When evening comes, barn owls take over where the harriers and other birds of prey have left off, covering the marshy pastureland and heath on pale, silent wings in search of voles and shrews, while nightjars churr from the low vegetation.

Late spring is when the heathland is at its best. Recently arrived whinchats warble their complex song from the fence stakes that mark out the edge of the grazing land, and the air shimmers over the golden banks of gorse as stonechats sing from the gorse stems; they seem to prefer burnt stems free of any spikes. Whinchats are migrants, but the related stonechats are resident on the Landes (heathlands) in all but the hardest weather, when they are driven to softer pastures. The wheatears that dash about the grassy tussocks in a mating dance, that encompasses their entire territory, are also summer visitors, as are the willow warblers and chiffchaffs that throng the goat willow thickets and stunted oaks, coming to take advantage of ample nests sites and abundant food generated by the reserve and the surrounding countryside.

The insect fauna is good with marsh fritillary butterflies, silver-studded blue butterflies and a large number and variety of heathland species of dragonflies and damselflies. The *libellula* species of dragonflies are abundant on the marshy ground and their larvae feed on tadpoles and the larvae of tiny fish and insects that live in the pools and streams. *Libellula quadri-maculata* otherwise known as the 'four-spotted chaser' is common here as is the blue *libellula*, similar in shape and size and known as the 'broad-bodied chaser'. These insects wait in ambush on reed stems and tussock grass, dashing out to capture passing flies and other insects.

The acid soil and high water content dissolves out nutrients and minerals, and the need for plants to supplement their meagre diet with high nitrogen food is taken to the ultimate level by insect-eating plants like sundews. The lures are sticky and flower-like and trap flies, beetles and bees. The top of the flower is red with a number of hairs, each one tipped with a ball of sticky resin. As the insect lands, its legs become entangled; the plant covers the insect with sticky threads and digests it.

Darter dragonfly (Libellula depressa): *An ambush hunter usually found perched on strategically placed reeds from which it flies out to catch flying insects*

Heathland is not rich in mammals although, where the ground is not so wet, shrews and hedgehogs are abundant. The acidity of the soil precludes the presence of a large number of earthworms; they prefer the farmed pasture adjoining the reserve, as do moles. Weasels, stoats, beech martens and European polecats prey on the mice and voles that periodically enjoy population explosions due to a variety of environmental and seasonal factors. However, these eruptions are short-lived as the increased numbers soon exceed the availability of green food and seeds.

Cragou is part of an exciting experiment, a new partnership between the SEPNB (Société pour l'Etude et la Protection de la Nature en Bretagne) and the local farming community, a productive initiative that has been good for wildlife and farming alike. The heathland is grazed throughout the year by Dartmoor ponies and Nantes cows, both breeds able to thrive on poor forage. The management plan depends on a small number of animals cropping a relatively large acreage of land so that the diversity of wild flowering plants, grasses and sedges is kept in equilibrium with no species becoming dominant. If the

Cragou: Maintained by grazing with cattle and Dartmoor ponies, this area of moorland, heath and dwarf woodland holds a wealth of specially adapted wildlife

Like a large swift, the hobby falcon (Falco subbuteo) *is a master of light*

herbage grows more thickly in one area, the animals congregate to reap the bounty and the balance is maintained.

Indeed, the survival of this considerable and important heathland is due to this farming/conservation partnership. In the past Breton farmers made good use of the heathland; it was valuable sheep pasture and the wetland areas were good for fattening cattle, but the number of animals that can be sustained by heathland and bog is limited. This fact, together with other social and economic factors, led to the conversion of most acid heaths from purely grazing to arable and conifer plantation. Happily, financial assistance from the EU and market-driven incentives such as the growing demand for organic and holistically-produced animal and plant-based foods has provided the impetus to return to farming methods that do not need such intensive chemical assistance and has brought about a more diverse system of farming with a wider variety of crops.

This movement towards conversion of land formerly under intensive management to organic agriculture and horticulture has meant that there is now every reason for preserving and enhancing some of the best features of the northern French countryside. Cragou is a good example of the way in which conservation and productive land management can go hand in hand for mutual benefit.

Parc Naturel Régional d'Armorique (Ile d'Ouessant [Ushant] & Archipel de Molène)

Off the coast of the Brest Peninsula a group of islands and rocky spurs guard the Western Approaches to the Channel with a devastating array of wild granite teeth. The Ile d'Ouessant and the Molène archipelago form a priceless Biosphere Reserve recognised by UNESCO as a maritime habitat of world importance. One of the most remote areas of Brittany, this outlying part of the Parc Naturel Régional d'Armorique can be reached by boat from Brest or, more conveniently, by the shorter route from Le Conquet.

Of the eight islands, (Balanec, Bannec, Béniguet, Litiry, Quéménès, Molène, Trielen and Ouessant), Ouessant (Ushant) is the largest, at eight kilometres long by three kilometres across. It has no natural harbour where a fishing fleet might anchor. Deprived of a living from fishing, the skills of the hardy Breton seafarers were put to the test in the merchant fleets of France and other European seafaring countries. While the men were at sea wives and daughters established a matriarchy running the home and farming the few acres of productive land. Legend has it that the island women developed their own social system and control over their lives and their farms, and that they chose and proposed marriage to eligible bachelors. Closer to the mainland, Molène is the only other permanently inhabited island.

The danger posed by these islands is measured in the number of the lighthouses and radar beacons that perch on the rocks like brightly coloured cormorants. The 180 ft high black and white tower at Creac'h on Ushant was built in the middle of the 19th century and its lamp, first lit in 1863, was famed as the most powerful in the world. What effect it had on the millions of migrating birds that pass to and fro this archipelago is not known. But, today the bird observatory, hard by the Creac'h

Cormorant
(Phalacrocorax carbo)*:
Perfectly adapted to fish
in deep water,
cormorants are
frequently seen on
sunny rocks with their
wings outstretched,
drying their plummage*

lighthouse, is invaluable for the study of bird migration, both in early spring and during the gale-prone October passage of migrant birds.

Thirty species of birds breed on the islands, including lesser and greater black-blacked gulls, herring gull, storm petrel, shags, cormorants, guillemots, and razorbills. On Ouessant, one of Europe's rarest crows, the chough, plays on the wind and can sometimes be seen from the Centre Ornithologique at Calgrac'h, at one end of the Baie de Béninou.

*The turbulent seas around this coast provide perfect
fishing grounds for guillemots* (Uria aalge)

Rosemary (Rosmarinus officinalis)*: Medicinal and culinary herb, rich in nectar and a favourite with bees, frequently found beside the ruins of long abandoned cottages*

It is as an observatory for passage migrants and rare vagrant birds that these islands come into their own. Each year rare warblers from as far afield as Siberia and North America are blown in and take advantage of the opportunity to rest for a short while before trying to find their way back to their breeding or wintering grounds.

The larger islands are covered with a thin layer of acid soil. This does not allow for the economic growth of crops, so just a few sheep and horses are left to graze the maritime turf. Heathland, the natural habitat of the islands, is gradually recolonising the land and the wild heathland flowers provide a marvellous backdrop to birdwatching in the spring.

Of course, birds are not the only attraction among this scatter of hard rock shards and thrift-topped islands. The mixture of ocean currents brings nutrients to the surface that encourages a growth of minute phytoplankton and zooplankton.

These microscopic forms of life are the foundation layer of the sea's ecological pyramid. The abundance of food promotes a wealth of sea life with small fish feeding larger fish and so on until the mammals take their turn. The surrounding sea is well known as a gathering place for Atlantic bottlenose dolphins and grey seals and a small population of European otters that hunt for butterfish in the wrack beds.

This rough, isolated, sometimes desolate, sometimes dramatically beautiful part of Brittany deserves its status as a Biosphere Reserve, a designation that is only bestowed on the most important sites in terms of wildlife species and habitat.

Pointe de Mousterlin & Kermor Plage

In the very south of Finistère, the land between Quimper and Lorient is known as the Pays de Bigouden and at the eastern end, between Pont l'Abbé and Beg Meil Head a large bay, the Anse de Bénodet, attracts much wildlife as well as summer tourists. The Pointe de Mousterlin is one of many excellent places to watch for wildlife and it's easy to find. Take the D44 from Bénodet heading towards Fouesnant and at Le Perguet branch off onto the D134, which leads straight to the Pointe. Alternatively, pick up the D145 from Fouesnant, which joins the D134.

Between the Pointe de Mousterlin and Beg Miel Head four kilometres of splendid beaches are stretched out for the holiday-maker's delight. A few remnants of concrete gun emplacements, left over from the Second World War sit, half-submerged in the sand, their foundations undermined by the sea and over half a century of Atlantic gales – incongruous relics of the past like the half-buried statue of the great King Ozymandias in Shelley's poem:-

'My name is Ozymandias, king of kings:
Look on my works, ye mighty, and despair!'
Nothing beside remains. Round the decay
Of that colossal wreck, boundless and bare,
The lone and level sands stretch far away.

It doesn't matter how great or how wonderful the structure, eventually nature will break it down – statue, mountain or gun emplacement.

The beaches are backed by dunes of fine pale shelly sand held together against the wind by the long fibrous roots of marram grass, which prevents the dunes from marching inland. Dunes can be badly affected by the wind. The architect of all beaches and dune systems, the wind will etch out a weak spot causing a 'blow' (a rupture along the front edge of the dune.) The effect can be minor as with an erosion gully or, in the case of an Atlantic gale, it can be catastrophic with a huge area of dunes being swept inland to cover more mature habitats behind the dune bank with a smothering blanket of sand; it will take many years to revegetate. These 'blows' are most often triggered in areas where the holding grasses have been damaged or killed by wheeled vehicles, human feet or horses' hooves. Efforts have been made to reinstate the marram grass plantations, which have been fenced off for their own protection, while wooden slatted paths have been laid though the dunes to avoid careless erosion of the sand.

Behind the dune system at Mousterlin, 177 hectares of polderland constitutes a natural treasure house. This partly flooded salt marsh controlled by an ancient system of dykes and sluices is well served with footpaths, some of which run for more than a kilometre before ending in a patch of scrub, a small plantation of mixed pines with an under-storey of bramble, or even a raised observation platform.

This enormous area of reed beds, willow and alder scrub is

*Mousterlin: Avenues of grass and trees run alongside
dune marshland rich in swallowtail butterflies
and birds, including Cetti's warbler*

owned and protected by CEL (Conservatoire de l'Espace
Littoral) and attracts an abundance of birds, mammals and
insects. The most obvious bird here is one that is heard rather
than seen. The Cetti's warbler makes its present felt by a powerful explosion of song – once heard, never mistaken. The bird
most often seen is the beautiful little egret and a large colony is
in residence all through the year. A substantial number of reed
warblers thrives in the phragmites reed beds and sedge warblers
sing from the willow and alder scrub throughout April and
May. Sedge warblers may look like their reed-nesting cousins,
but have a far more interesting song. In between the usual
churrs and twitters they copy phrases from willow warblers,
marsh warblers and blackcaps. Reed buntings are at their best
along the edge of the reed beds, the cock birds elegant in
strongly striated plumage and black and white heads. The reed
beds and the lee of the sedges are also home to water rails,
whose strange pig-like squall punctuates the day while coot and

moorhen bicker and squabble over nesting territories – floating their nests at the edge of the reeds like tiny rafts.

Where the land is drier, stands of pedunculate oak and Scots pine thrive. Many of the oaks have been planted by birds. Jays, in particular, store acorns for hard times by burying them in the soft acid soil. Most of the stored acorns are recovered and eaten during late autumn and winter, but some are left over and in spring throw up new shoots. Dune slack oaks are often limited in height. When they become taller than the dunes they become vulnerable to sudden gusts of wind off the sea. However, those oaks lucky enough to have seeded near Scots pine fare much better as the pines provide a wind break. These oak stands are a good place to see purple hairstreak butterflies in August and green woodpeckers all year round.

Further east, along the coast, is the Vallée de l'Odet where the river is bordered with woods of sweet chestnut and pine. River boats cruise from Bénodet to Quimper and there are several lovely walks. Other day-trips can be made by boat from Bénodet and Concarneau to the Iles des Glénan, a small group of protected islets that support a rich wildlife.

Between Bénodet and Pont l'Abbé, Kermor Plage, another enormous stretch of sandy beach, is backed by dunes, carved and cut on the seaward side by the prevailing wind. Into some of the more compacted sand banks, sand martins have built large colonies, the tunnels pitting the sand like a Gruyère cheese. At present these delicate birds seem able to cope with the impact of tourists on the beach during the summer. Perhaps this is because the maximum disturbance, mid-July through August, comes at the end of their breeding season.

The sheer scale of the beach between Pont l'Abbé and Beg Meil head makes this a complex and challenging place to watch the waders that stream in on autumn and winter migration, but this should not be regarded as a negative aspect – just take one area at a time. Feeding parties of migrant 'peeps' (tiny waders like sanderling, knot, dunlin, turnstones and little stint) scurry like clockwork toys ahead of the advancing wavelets and among the larger waders redshank, curlew, ruff and the curlew-like whimbrel gather in favoured spots along the beach. Telescope or binoculars are essential here. Along some of the beaches steps have been built at intervals to protect the dunes from erosion: they provide an excellent place to watch the sea for skuas and terns.

Evidence of the productivity of the surrounding shallow sea can also be seen in the huge number and variety of seashells (empty of course) of many species found on the beach. However, the vast number of empty shells on the beach indicates the abundant supply of full shells, either in the sea itself, or burrowed into the beach, and this potential food supply is the main attraction for birds and for fish

The whole of this region is marvellous because of the variety and diversity of habi-

Swallowtail butterfly (Papilio machaon): *Largest and most beautiful of the European butterflies – a creature of damp marshy habitats*

Fennel (Foeniculum vulgare): *A wild plant with medicinal and culinary uses – it goes well with fish. One of the food plants of the swallowtail butterfly*

Previous pages: *Marsh frog on frog bit* (Rana ridibunda): *Large, colourful and noisy, these frogs sound like ducks quacking on the edge of a pond*
Opposite: *Brimstone butterfly* (Gonepteryx rhamni): *This is the butter-coloured-fly from which the name 'butterfly' originated*
Above: *Red hawker dragonfly* (Sympetrum striolatum): *A common dragonfly often found in a sandy habitat near dune slacks (pools)*

tats. The presence of large numbers of European swallow-tail butterflies, marsh and edible frogs, and a multitude of dragon-flies in the dune slacks and in the drained areas behind is an added bonus – the butterflies and dragonflies can be seen on the beaches too. The dunes and marshes impart a feeling of peace-fulness and though at first sight the dunes might appear desert-like, a second look will show the abundance and productivity to be found within, enough to keep the naturalist happy and occu-pied for far longer than the average holiday-time allows.

Towns and Villages

Bénodet

Sitting on the banks of the estuary of the river Odet, and looking out onto the Atlantic, Bénodet was once an important fishing and trading port in the days when Quimper was at its most influential. Known as one of the most beautiful estuaries in Brittany, and still a favoured site for historic sailing ships, it is dominated by a lighthouse that appears to rise up out of the middle of the tiers of old fishermen's cottages, some of which have been converted into holiday accommodation. The newer part of the town spreads up the hill to a variety of municipal buildings and the tourist office.

In the 18th and 19th centuries, Bénodet and Ste Maxine, a little fishing village on the opposite bank of the estuary, were two separate entities. Now joined by a tall new bridge, both can boast of the excellence of their seafood restaurants.

A number of *vedettes* (day-trip boats) ply the beautiful riverscape from Bénodet to Quimper which, in the past, tempted the invading Vikings and the Spanish navy anxious to enjoy its riches for themselves. But their attempts to navigate the Odet were thwarted by nature. Just before the river reaches Quimper it narrows and a sharp bend between hard granite rocks squeezes the fast-flowing current. The invaders considered it to be too dangerous to continue and were forced to turn back.

One of the most popular resorts in southern Brittany,

Bénodet is never crowded (except perhaps in August) and it's well placed as a base for exploring the Bigouden country. A favourite with writers and artists, such notables as Marcel Proust, Emile Zola and Sarah Bernhardt have all stayed here.

Concarneau

Modern Concarneau is an important fishing port – indeed the third largest in France – but it is the 14th century historic core (the Ville Close) that the tourists come to see. Konk Kerné is Breton for 'inlet of Cornouaille' and the walled town, once a fortress, is built on a rocky island sitting in the middle of this inlet, dominating the harbour. Today it's a bustle of tourist shops and restaurants, but despite commercialisation, the walls enclose a scrap of history and a fascinating glimpse of the past.

The ramparts and double gateway speak of a time when this part of Brittany was prey to brigands. The deep-water harbour and the bay beyond would have been a tempting prize for opportunist raiders, but when the tide is full the walls present a formidable face to any attacker. These days it's a pleasure to walk around the ramparts and look down onto the old buildings inside and out to the port beyond.

Opposite the entrance to the old walled town is a large market where all kinds of Breton delicacies are on sale, from fish and oysters to locally grown fruit and vegetables. And the town, both new and old, is well served with dozens of excellent restaurants offering fish as fresh as it's possible to get short of catching it yourself.

This is a delightful little corner of Brittany with several fine sandy beaches on the far side of the Pointe de Caballou peninsula. The Bretons love to dress up in their national costume, play their distinctive music and display their prowess in the local step dances; two festivals here, one at the end of July and another in August, show them at their best.

Locronan

Roman Polański used this pretty town as a backdrop for his film *Tess of the d'Urbevilles* and the old cobbled square of perfectly preserved Renaissance houses, complete with dormers and timbering, does have a feel of Hardy's brooding Dorset. At the lower end of the square, the whole of which is designated an historic monument, once stood the headquarters of the French East India Company, destined to founder as the British dominated the far eastern trade. Dominating the square is the splendid 15th-century granite church of St Ronan. The spire was struck by lightening so many times it was replaced by a turret during the 19th century.

In the early days Locronan was a centre for flax-spinning, which gradually developed into a major sail-cloth industry supplying the merchant fleets and navies of half of Europe, including Britain. The demise of the East India Company, combined with a decree by Louis XIV that ended the monopoly on sail-cloth, deprived the town of its vast income, and the economy collapsed. However, although the town's present prosperity mainly derives from tourists attracted to the magnificent old buildings, they also come to buy from the many local artists and weavers.

Up to the 18th and even the early part of the 19th centuries the woodlands around the town were full of wolves, with the citizens unable to defend their flocks of sheep and cattle from these powerful animals. Sadly today there are no wolves within 700 or 800 miles and much of the forest cover has been felled.

Pont Aven

The river Aven is characterised by the mill leats that impound the water on its way to the sea. It was once said that Pont Aven had 14 mills and 15 houses. It was the most important of all the corn-milling towns of the region.

In the late 19th century the 'new' railway from Paris opened up the area and its beauty turned Pont Aven into an artists' settlement. They came in their droves to find inspiration in the quiet villages, along the dramatic coastline and in the nearby lovely Bois d'Amour, which has been much painted. Victor Hugo and Flaubert were regular visitors and attics and lofts around the town were rented to artists – one of whom was Paul

Pont Aven: Quaint, pretty artists' colony, once the home of Paul Gauguin, Victor Hugo, Chateaubriand and Flaubert – among many others

Gauguin – leader of a group of Impressionists who lodged at the Gloanec, while another group known as Academics lived in the plush surroundings of the Hôtel Julia.

The museum, housed in the town hall, displays the history of the Pont-Aven School of artists with additional exhibitions of work by Gauguin. To reach it you have to cross a quaint little bridge, which looks as if it's made from large logs, but is actually reinforced concrete.

It's easy to see why Pont Aven is so popular. The river, tidal up as far as the town, runs along the main street and has been impounded, in the most attractive way, to drive the mills, many of which are now cafés, restaurants, hotels, art galleries and shops selling the traditional delicious *Traou Mad* biscuits. However, it's still the province of artists – the choice of work ranges from the traditional to the ultra modernist – and inspiring scenes meet the eye almost anywhere you care to rest an easel, even below the town where a footpath runs beside the river out towards to the sea, which is hidden from view behind tall wooded cliffs.

Pont l'Abbé

The historic capital of the area known as the Bigouden country, the name of this town derives from the order of monks that built the first bridge across the river inland from the estuary – the Pons Abatis. The monks of Loctudy are long since passed into history, but a typical Bigouden farm has been restored to show what life was like for some of the people who lived here.

The local museum, in the 13th-century castle, houses traditional costumes and a collection of the sugar-loaf head-dresses of the women of the region – so tall they became known as Eckmühl lighthouses. This region was a centre for a cottage industry in embroidery and lace-making that produced works of incredible beauty and diversity. Every town appeared to have its own particular style of costume both for men and for women. Exhibitions in the castle show marvellous examples of modern lace-work and embroidery as well as the wedding dress and costumes of past times and in July there are large festivals dedicated to the *brodeuses* (embroiderers) with additional exhibitions throughout the region and large musical gatherings where Celtic music (including bagpipes) is played in the streets followed by people wearing their intricate local costumes.

At the front of the castle is a large square of open water, the holding reservoir for a still functional ancient tidal mill. The gates open and close to control the flow of water through the wheel. The waters of this impounded lake are much appreciated by the local cormorants and a large flock of duck of mixed parentage showing indications of cross breeding with domestic duck and wild mallard.

FURNELL

Ille et Vilaine

Little owl

Introduction

The department of Ille et Vilaine is bordered to the east by Normandy, to the west by Côtes d'Armor and Morbihan and in the south by Loire Atlantique. Of all the departments that make up the region of Brittany it has the smallest coastline by far – barely 50 kilometres long. Even so it is delightfully varied, stretching from Le Mont St Michel in the east to St Briac sur Mer at the mouth of the river Frémur.

Shielded by the Cotentin Peninsula from the worst of the winter's shrill easterly winds and tides that tear down the English Channel from the North Sea, the Baie du Mont St Michel was a favoured anchorage in the days of sailing ships and oared galleys. The deep sheltered estuaries of rivers like the Rance provided ideal moorings for trade between the Bronze Age and Iron Age inhabitants of Britain and France, a link that continues to this day with the busy ferry port at St Malo.

During the Second World War the beautiful walled city of St Malo, which sits at the mouth of the river Rance, was devastated by bombing, but the people showed amazing fortitude and skill in rebuilding it – so much so that it is hard to realise that the medieval town is not the untouched original. Over the centuries, the Bretons endured many conflicts and built themselves the harbour at St Malo because it is well protected from the

Sheep, Mont St Michel

seaward side by a number of rocky islets. This anchorage developed over hundreds of years and by the 17th century had become the foremost trading port in France. The rocky islets were fortified as a deterrent to invaders until the development of powerful ship-borne guns – and this change in naval armament turned many of the once impregnable fortifications into interesting ruins where seabirds find ample nesting ledges.

The river Rance itself has a large rise and fall of tides, a natural phenomenon exploited in the 20th century to generate electricity. However, these full tides made it difficult for inexperienced sailors to navigate the river and the sandbars, a characteristic exploited by the corsairs or privateers who engaged in the trade known as 'la Course' (piracy). The sailors who hailed from St Malo were bold and fierce, sailing out on the tide to harry ships, steal the cargo and rob the crews of valuables. This 'trade' made the town even richer and increased the reputation of its seafaring men. Indeed, during the reign of Louis XIV the trade of privateer was given official sanction when these men were able to assist the French navy in attacking ships, particularly English ships, during one of the many conflicts waged between the two countries.

Up until the late 19th century the deep ocean fishermen of the little port of Dinard, on the opposite bank of the river Rance to St Malo, spread their nets as far north as the Newfoundland Banks for the trade in salt cod, but in the late Victorian period the pretty village was discovered by tourists from both sides of the Channel. It is now one of the most popular holiday towns in northern France, which is not at all surprising as the sandy beaches and spectacular coastline, particularly the Pointe du Décollé, has provided a wealth of inspiration for artists and musicians – most notably Claude Debussy.

To the east of St Malo, and around the Pointe de Grouin to Cancale (world renowned for the quality of its oysters) is mile upon mile of fine sandy beaches interspersed with headlands topped with low-growing grasses. Carry on to Dol de Bretagne, 'Capital of the Marshes'. Once an island in the sea it now lies several miles inland. Indeed, fascinating as this short stretch of coast may be, the vast majority of the department of Ille et Vilaine lies in the Argoat, an inland countryside of heaths and woods and productive farmland. Tens of millions of years ago this beautiful region was part of a majestic range of mountains that ran like a spine across the whole of north-west France. Time and the elements have eroded the mighty peaks to stumps of mineral-rich hard igneous rock, granite and schists, flowing with rivers like the

Southern marsh orchid (Dactylorhiza praetermissa)*: Grows on lime-rich marshland, particularly in the lee of old sand dunes. They are not common, but there is just the possibility of seeing one in the area*

Vilaine, from which the department takes its name. The rivers were the abrasive agents that brought about the fall of the mountain range, literally wearing it away, and the erosion of these ancient rocks created immense areas of free-draining, basically infertile sandy soils. In time, plants and animals adapted to exploit these unique conditions and heaths and acid woodland of oak, Scots pine, ash and lime developed to cover the land. Some of it has since been commercially planted with sweet chestnut.

In the early Bronze Age the megalith builders decorated their land, indeed the whole of Brittany, with chamber tombs, menhirs and alignments using huge stones, some weighing nearly 100 tons. Today the megaliths are most often associated with areas of forest such as the so-called Druid's Ring in the Forêt de Fougères, north-east of Fougères itself – an alignment of ten menhirs and a gallery tomb – and the Roche aux Fées, a group of 40 huge boulders of red shale that lie beside the Etang de Marcillé Robert. From Rennes take the D41 south towards Janzé. Continue on this road until the sign for Retiers (D47). At Retiers turn on to the D107.

Many farms still display remnants of ancient fortifications. Most of them are now no more than grassy mounds, but their presence speaks of a history of continuous danger from war and invasion. During the years at the end of the first millennium daily life was disrupted by the incursions of marauding Norsemen and Vikings, navigating their longships into the heartlands of the Ille et Vilaine down the rivers Rance and Cousenon. They came. They saw. They liked what they saw and they stayed to found a new dynasty of ruling warlords, the Normans. Their history is bound tightly to the domination of northern France and eventual conquest of England by William of Normandy in 1066.

The contrast between coast and countryside could not be more marked. The area around Rennes, capital of the department of Ille et Vilaine and administrative capital of Brittany, is dominated by deep river valleys, tall escarpments, marvellous forests and wildlife-rich marshland. Modern-day Rennes is a busy bustling city, the hub of nine major roads that stretch out in all directions across Brittany and into the rest of France. Of the other main towns in the region, Fougères and Vitré are the largest, but away from the bustle of these towns (and there are few large towns in this department) there is a sense of peacefulness. Trees and birds dominate the ancient landscape which, at any season of the year, is extremely beautiful. In spring, the land is flushed with green and the blossom of multitudes of wild shrubs and flowering trees, and takes on the texture and colours of a French Impressionist painting. In autumn, the effect is even further enhanced when the leaves turn to glorious red and gold.

Wildlife

Cancale & Coast

The D201 scenic route from St Malo to Cancale 'par la côte' also forms part of the GR 34 (Grande Randonée) – one of the systems of waymarked walks that criss-cross the whole of the French countryside.

Cancale itself is world renowned for seafood, particularly oysters. Sitting in the lee of the Pointe du Grouin, the small town is fronted by the Baie du Mont St Michel where the oysters grow in natural, but carefully managed, conditions. Indeed the whole of this bay is given over to the farming of shellfish, which reaches industrial proportions with thousands of oyster beds and a forest of wooden posts – the nursery for millions of mussels – stretching over 22 kilometres of the bay.

The Pointe du Grouin, a granite bulwark just to the north of Cancale, juts out into the waters of the Channel. Its effective-ness as a breakwater for winds and tides up the Western Approaches is enhanced by the Ile des Landes, 21 hectares of granite and schist angled north-east as if turned by the power of the sea. One of the oldest bird sanctuaries in Brittany, the

Oystercatcher (Haematopus ostralegus) *and grey plover* (Pluvialis squatarola): *The rich sandy mud is full of worms and abundant shellfish, such as crabs, providing wonderful feeding for these birds*

whole island was designated a nature reserve in 1958 and now comes under the protection of SEPNB (Société pour l'Etude et la Protection de la Nature en Bretagne). A considerable population of breeding birds, particularly cormorant, shelduck, oyster-catcher and, of course, herring gulls, depends on the safety and peace and quiet they find here. In spring and autumn the usual population of birds is augmented by migrants from Britain as terns move north or south depending on the season. In spring the Arctic terns leave Britain for the Antarctic and the common, little and sandwich terns head for the West African coast. In autumn they make the return journey.

The area is suitable for growing shellfish because of its geological history. The slow rise of the level of the sea following the last Ice Age, which created the English Channel and connected the Atlantic Ocean and North Sea, also affected the many rivers that flow to the sea in this region. Low-lying river floodplains were inundated as the sea rose to its present level, and the influence of the tides was felt in the estuaries, causing a back-up of silt and the creation of mud and sand flats and level salt marshland. This is just the sort of habitat favoured by wildfowl and waders – and has proved ideal too for the cultivation of shellfish in the nutrient-rich waters.

Follow the D201 from Cancale to the Pointe du Grouin and its lighthouse (there is an excellent view from here.) The Ile des Landes is on your right. The road then heads west towards St Malo along a coastline of rugged rocks and small bays backed by a dune system and marshes at l'Anse du Verger. It is unique in the whole of the department of Ille et Vilaine and a known resting place for a large number of small bird migrants, including willow warbler, chiffchaff, garden warbler, redstart and pied flycatcher, which pause here before crossing the Channel to breed in Britain and further north.

The dune slacks (small pools of water trapped behind the dunes) support a fascinating array of amphibians and attract

Little egret (Egretta garzetta)*: A common small heron often seen along the shallow margins of the Baie*

reptiles such as adders, grass snakes, common lizards and sand lizards in abundance. The slacks also attract larger bird migrants and little egrets and, occasionally, a white stork may be seen fishing in the shallow water. Black terns, whiskered terns, common and Arctic terns and parties of little terns also visit the marshes, and in spring cement their pair bonds with a charming display when the males approach the females, shuffling along with drooped wings and a gift of a small fish held in the beak.

The prime plant of dune habitat is the deep-rooted marram grass. This member of the grass family is vital to the stability of the entire dune system. Its widespread, net-like root system holds the loose grains of sand together. In time the dead plant material collects up against the grass stems, which can stand a metre high, creating small areas of fertility that are then colonised by leguminous plants like sea pea and birds foot trefoil. Gorse is another plant that helps to consolidate the dunes and provide nest sites for linnets and Dartford warblers, whitethroats and dunnocks.

Dune orchids and southern marsh orchids are rare, but they do occur here. In August large numbers of clouded yellow butterflies, and the closely related pale clouded yellow butterflies, gather on the flowers of sea holly and jostle with red admiral and painted lady butterflies. If the wind is off the land for more than a day or two these insects will migrate across the Channel and turn up on Chesil Beach in Dorset and on coastal meadowlands in Hampshire and Sussex.

The presence of rabbits is always an incentive to the smaller predatory mammals such as beech martens, stoats and weasels

Insects on knapweed (greater knapweed – Centuarea scabiosa):
A superb nectar plant for bumble bees, butterflies and
day-flying moths. Grows in the lea of dunes where
pulverised sea shells provide a limestone soil

as well as foxes, and the dunes are also home to large colonies of natterjack toads that spawn in the fugitive brackish dune pools.

The large number of empty seashells adds to the fertility of the dunes and the landward side of the dune system has been covered with a dense mat of low growing, rabbit-nibbled turf, an ideal habitat for beetles and other small winged invertebrates as well as velvet ants and colonies of red ants. Dune systems and marshes are rare habitats these days and dwindling fast, which is a great shame as they are full of marvellous natural history surprises.

Baie du Mont St Michel

The Baie du Mont St Michel is bounded to the east by the huge land mass of the Cotentin Peninsula, to the west by Pointe de Grouin and on the landward side by the estuary of the river Couesnon. In the distant past, about 18,000 years ago, when the European ice sheet was relaxing its grip, the huge melting glaciers produced a welter of water, thick with a slurry of pulverised rock. This mass of melting ice caused the sea level to rise and the result was a breach in the land bridge between Britain and Europe – known today in Britain as the English Channel and in France as La Manche.

The higher ground and hard rocks of the Cotentin Peninsula remained above water, creating a unique system of currents that carried silt into the once deep valley, forming a series of salt marsh lands bisected by the river Couesnon and fronted by an immense shallow bay. The soil is alluvial silt brought by tides and the wind and the several rivers that empty their waters here, feeding the silt and nutrients into the flow across the bay.

The most important part of this natural triumvurate (the sea, the land and the rivers) is the sea in the shape of the Channel,

Salt marsh, Mont St. Michel

which adds its own mix of minerals and nutrients, thus helping to create a wonderland for the small invertebrates and crustaceans that live in the mud, and indeed for the birds that flock here in their millions during the winter and on spring and autumn passage.

Humankind has thrived in this region for 10,000 years or more, particularly so because of the rocky outcrop known as Mont Tombe. Joined to the mainland by a causeway, it rises from the dark chocolate-coloured mud a mere kilometre out from the shoreline. Land reclamation and the diversion of the river Couesnon to accommodate agriculture have had a dramatic effect on the deposits of sand and silt, as the diverted river system is no longer able to carry the silt out to sea. The causeway itself is part of the problem too, upsetting the natural swirl of currents in the bay and causing the area around the Mont to silt up. Plans are afoot to remove the causeway and replace it with a structure that offers less resistance to the tides; but this will cause other problems for the people who live and work on the rock, in the terraces of attractive old buildings that now house gift and craft shops, cafés and restaurants.

However, it is vital that the build up of silt should be dealt with, albeit as considerately as possible for the human population. The consequences of doing nothing would be disastrous for the copious wildlife that depends on this area.

The bay of Mont St Michel is best divided into three habitat types – marine, littoral and polder (salt marsh). The latter holds the greater number and species of wild birds; in winter tens of thousands of lapwings, curlew, godwits, together with huge mixed flocks of sandpipers, knot, sanderling and turnstones, fly to and fro along the polders and the tide line. These polders are renowned for the sheep that graze on them; the meat is a speciality of the region, considered a delicacy because of the slightly salty, gamey flavour. The sheep have other uses too, keeping the turf short and in perfect order for the waders that roost here at high tide, and for Brent geese and enormous flocks of widgeon and pintail that graze the salty grass. Shelduck can be seen all year; they breed in the holes that pit the turf on the sea walls and on the banks of the river Couesnon.

Kestrel (Falco tinnunculus): *A mouse-hunting falcon of open grassland. Often found nesting in human habitation and in hollow trees*

Such a large number of prey species attracts wintering peregrine falcons, and in spring and summer the common buzzards that are present over the bay all year are joined by marsh, hen and Montagu's harrier. The harriers breed nearby, but hunt and display over the polder land.

The wide, open spaces and salt marshes provide a happy hunting ground for kestrels, the grassland being rich in vole species.

The littoral, the tidal zone between sea and polder, and the marine habitat are constantly changing because of the twice-daily inundation of the tides. This closes off the invertebrate food from the wading birds for several hours but allows other species to take advantage of the fish and small fry that follow the incoming waters. Common terns, sandwich terns and little terns plunge-dive for food. The cormorants that nest on nearby rocky outcrops harvest the running tide, as do grey herons and little egrets. All benefit from the movement of the water, which drives some of the smaller flat fish out of their hiding places.

However, the area around Mont St Michel is not all about seabirds. On the Mont itself, in and around the buildings, are a number of species that have learned to benefit from humankind. Apart from the ubiquitous feral pigeon, stock doves, and collared doves, perky black redstarts nest in the walls, and the mud below the gates near the causeway is just the right consistency to provide building material for swallows and house martins. It's a pleasure to watch them at such unusually close quarters as they swoop down to the muddy puddles. Unrelated, but equally at home in the air, common European swifts nest in the roof spaces of the ancient houses and religious buildings and fly about in screaming parties, hundreds strong, on summer evenings.

The plant growth on the polders is affected by the sheep; indeed many of the grass species have been encouraged because of centuries of grazing. The most noticeable flowering plants are pink thrift and sea lavender, with sea purslane and samphire colouring the margins of the marshes red and green. Away from the polders, where the river water dilutes the salt, beautiful purple loosestrife lines the banks.

Such an immense open expanse, in some places as much as 500 hectares of unbroken salt grasslands, allows for an interesting butterfly population, with a few dark green fritillaries in high summer and quite large numbers of European swallowtail butterflies along the ditches where they find nectar flowers and larval food plants for the caterpillars. Small white butterflies and Bath white butterflies are relatively common in high summer, in company with meadow brown, ringlet and grayling butterflies. Several of the blue butterflies are present in June, July and August too, mainly common blues and brown argus butterflies with a number of long-tailed blues. The map butterfly is not common here, but might be seen along the edge of the landward

Common blue butterfly male showing upper wing surface

side of the salt marsh. The map butterfly and its close relative, the small tortoiseshell butterfly, lay their eggs on the leaves of nettles, and this is a good place to look for the adults as well as the larvae.

The number and species of mammals depend on the available food. Rabbits, of course, are able to find ample grazing, but the open aspect of the land makes them vulnerable to aerial predators like common buzzards. Smaller mammals include weasel and stoat and the occasional otter. The shallow bay is the haunt of common and grey seals, though persecution because of fishing interests has led these creatures to be wary of humankind.

The saltings also support a large population of amphibians, particularly natterjack toads that find the warm, brackish water in the pools to their liking. Marsh frogs, on the other hand, prefer less salty water and are usually found in ditches that hold rainwater or run off from land drainage. Their raucous quacking calls are one of the typical sounds of Brittany's countryside.

Forêt Domaniale de Rennes

Described in many guidebooks as being on the doorstep of the historic city of Rennes, in reality this forest lies to the north east of the city and is one of four large areas of woodland. The Forêt Domaniale de Rennes itself is the largest, the Forêt de Chevré lies slightly to the east, the Forêt de St Aubin de Cormier to the north and the smallest block is the Forêt de Liffré. All are fragments of an ancient woodland that in the middle ages covered an immense triangle of land between the rivers Rance and Vilaine with Rennes at the apex. The forest is well supplied with footpaths and several small lakes are dotted throughout, the largest of these being the Etang du Maffrais, not far from St Sulpice la Forêt.

Bisected by the N12 from Rennes to Fougères, the Forêt

Domaniale de Rennes is a mixture of hardwood trees and plantation conifers covering some 3,000 hectares; it is famous for birds, particularly warblers and redstarts, woodpeckers and woodlarks. The mammal population is typical of this type of mixed woodland, with red squirrels, pine martens, beech martens, foxes and badgers. All are shy and must be watched carefully if they are not to take fright – true also for the roe deer, which are present here in some numbers.

Pearl-bordered fritillary butterfly (Boloria euphrosyna)*: A woodland butterfly declining over the whole of its European range. The larvae feed on violets*

The variety of butterfly species too is very much what you would expect to find in such a large area of mixed woodland, with white admiral and pearl-bordered fritillary butterflies as well as speckled wood and wall butterflies. The moth fauna is largely unexplored, but indications are that it should be rich in species.

About 20 kilometres north of Rennes the N12 crosses the north-western tip of the oak forest of Liffré, 1,000 hectares of ancient woodland rich in

Wall brown butterfly (Lasiommata megera) *and small copper butterfly* (Lycaena Phlaeas) *on Tansy. Usually found on rough grassland, these two butterflies depend on bright warm sunshine*

small birds and birds of prey, particularly honey buzzard and sparrowhawk and a small population of goshawk. Common buzzard certainly breed here. Again, as one would expect from such an enormously productive habitat, the mammals include badger, fox and fallow and roe deer, rabbits, stoats, weasels, pine and beech martens and red squirrels.

Managed by the ONF (Office National des Forêts), the reserve is a site of particular botanical interest. It has several woodland orchid species, including early purple orchid, greater and lesser butterfly orchid in spring and common spotted orchid in summer. Summer will see purple emperor, white admiral, silverwashed and dark green fritillary butterflies and the particularly delicate wood white butterfly.

These four forests, so close together, represent a wonderful

White admiral butterfly (Limenitis camilla):
Floating along the open rides, this woodland
beauty lays eggs on honeysuckle

Designed by nature to hunt in woodland, the sparrowhawk (Accipiter nisus), *is a master of ambush*

area for wildlife thanks to their overall size and the mix of tree species dominated by oak. Several smaller country roads run through them, with two scenic routes running across either end of the Forêt de St Aubin de Cormier as well as the GR 37.

Pays de Vilaine (Site des Corbinières)

In the very south of the Ille et Vilaine department, on the borders of Morbihan and Loire Atlantique, the river Vilaine runs through a deep, imposing gorge. Between the towns of Guipry and Messac the river has cut down through some of the most

Bugle (Ajuga repans)*: Common along the margins of the woodlands of the Pays de Vilaine where the copper/green foliage and blue flowers carpet the ground. Once used as a remedy for snake-bite, the leaves have powerful antiseptic properties*

Gatekeeper butterfly (Pyronia tithonus)*: Also known as the hedge brown and often seen, as the name suggests, soaking up the sun on fences, walls and wooden gate rails where woodland meets farmland*

ancient rocks in France. Handsome trees clothe the steep-sided valley downstream as far as Langon.

This beautiful part of inland Brittany is a little off the beaten track, but well worth the effort it might take to find it. Take the D177 from Rennes to Pipriac and turn onto the D777 to Guipry. Alternatively take the N137/E3 Route Nationale from Rennes to Bain de Bretagne and turn onto the D772 to Messac. The GR 39 runs alongside the river in between these two towns on the Guipry side of the river.

The bedrock in this area is comprised of schists, foundations of an ancient and much-eroded mountain range. Oak, lime and ash trees cling to the valley side and in spring the air is full of birdsong, with redstart, willow warbler, garden warbler and blackcap. The warm updrafts provide good soaring conditions for flocks of swifts, swallows and martins and for common buzzards and honey buzzards, kestrels and jackdaws, not forgetting the occasional sparrowhawk, more obvious at dawn and in the late evening.

As the light fades so bats, a speciality of the gorge because of the ready availability of so many caves and crevices and the more than adequate food supply, begin to hunt. Some of the larger bats like Serrotine and greater and lesser horseshoe bats will range over many kilometres in search of insects to eat. The smaller bats such as Natterer's bats, brown long-eared bats and pipistrelle bats tend to hunt closer to the roost. It is because of the

Large white butterfly (Pierisbrassicae): The scientific name relates to the caterpillars' habit of eating leaves of cabbage and other brassicas – the primary food plant. Common all over the region

presence of so many of these fascinating nocturnal creatures that this area has been designated a nature reserve.

Pipistrelle bat (Pipistrellus pipistrellus): The smallest and most common of European bats. The closely related species Nathusius's pipistrelle (P. nathussi) is darker and slightly larger – only possible to identify in the hand

L'Ile aux Pies et le Grand Site Naturel de la Vallée de l'Oust (Bains sur Oust)

The river Oust is part of the Nantes–Brest Canal system, which runs through Redon, once a noted river port. This marvellous nature reserve, listed since 1900, lies to the north of Redon and is dominated by a massive granite cliff and escarpment, once a geological fault, which now constitutes the valley of the river Oust. The face of the escarpment is used by climbers for practice, and by soaring birds like buzzards, kestrels and jackdaws, as well as swifts, all revelling in the updraughts.

Take the D773 from Redon to La Gacilly. At Port Corbin turn off onto the D60 to Glénac. The marshes in this part of the valley of the river Oust are home in spring and summer to black

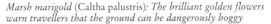

Marsh marigold (Caltha palustris)*: The brilliant golden flowers warn travellers that the ground can be dangerously boggy*

Eyed hawk moth (Smerinthus ocellata)*: Easily confused with the poplar hawk moth, this large moth often feeds on sallow and apple trees. Sallow is found in river valleys*

terns, grey herons, little egrets; and in winter their place is taken by large numbers of grebes, waders and rails. The GR 38 runs along the south bank of the river from Redon to Pont d'Oust before turning away southwards towards Peillac, and the section through the river valley is particularly attractive.

In spring the marsh also supports a considerable population of edible and marsh frogs, and several species of dragonflies. The butterfly fauna is augmented by European swallowtail and the marsh fritillary butterfly, and most of the commonplace European butterfly species are present. It may also be possible to locate the great raft spider in some of the quiet, undisturbed backwaters.

The river is popular with canoeists in spring and summer, but the scale of the area is such that there is always a quiet place for the naturalist.

Towns and Villages

Cancale

Split into two levels with the old port, La Houle, at the bottom of a long cobbled hill, the name Cancale is synonymous with oysters, and most of the fishermen's cottages along the sea front have been turned into superb seafood restaurants. The original inhabitants spoke a patois of their own and were particularly recognisable by their dark brown hair and Portuguese appearance. It was said they were descended from Portuguese mariners shipwrecked on the coast in the distant past, but it is more likely that their dark colouring came from the original Celtic inhabitants of the region.

The town has always been involved with fishing, though nowadays the deep sea trawler fleet has been abandoned in favour of earning a living from the shallow water of the Baie du Mont St Michel, which is perfect for mussel and oyster farming. Mussels are grown on oak posts hammered into the bed of the bay and occupy an area of over 120 square kilometres. The oysters are grown from spat (one-year-old oysters) brought in from the Charente coast and grown for three or four years on raised platforms in wire mesh containers that allow the sea to bring nutrients on the tide and wash away mud and pollution. The oyster beds can be seen at low tide from the sea front and harbour walls, and more can be learned about this fascinating occupation from the Museum of Oyster Farming on l'Aurore beach. In contrast to all this organised activity, just around the Pointe du Hock lies a nature reserve of dunes and old salt marsh.

Dinard

Situated on the west bank of the Rance Estuary, Dinard, known as the 'Nice of the North', owes its success to tourism. From a simple 19th-century fishing village it grew into a major holiday resort. Following the lead of an English woman who built a villa here, American tourists began to build villas along the cliffs too, and their example was soon copied by Parisians. Now the sea front and cliffs boast some lovely mock-Gothic and *belle époque* houses.

Wooded hillsides look down onto three superb sandy beaches and the estuary of the river Rance, and in the distance, on the

Dinard

far bank of the river, the walled city of St Malo. The temperature is controlled by the Gulf Stream that runs very close to the coast here and a great deal of sub-tropical vegetation has been planted by the villa owners. The Rance itself is renowned for sailing. The violent tides have been tamed by the construction of an electricity generating barrage across the mouth of this beautiful river. Day-trip boats ply inland as far as Dinan. It takes the best part of the day there and back and makes a marvellous outing.

Fougères

This frontier town achieved importance during the 11th century when a settlement grew up around the castle built originally to defend the Duchy of Brittany. The new town became an obvious symbol of the power of the weavers, dyers and cloth merchants and later, in the 15th century, the manufacture of linen brought considerable wealth. The skyline of the old quarter, known as the Bourg Neuf, is dominated by the Bell Tower, erected to celebrate the power of these merchants. This medieval part of Fougères is the heart of the town, with modern improvements including a theatre in the Italianate style built in 1886 and decorated with masks of tragedy and comedy.

The church of St Sulpice was begun in the 11th century and rebuilt during the 17th. It houses two medieval Breton altarpieces, a wooden statue of Notre Dame des Marais, the focus of a little-known cult, and some beautiful 16th-century stained glass designed by a local artist.

A museum dedicated to Emmanuel de la Villéon is housed in a splendid porched building in the Rue Nationale. De Villéon (1858–1944), one of the last Impressionists, loved nature and excelled in landscapes; nearly a hundred of his paintings are on show here.

In the 19th century the town was largely given over to industry and, up until the First World War was considered to be the world capital of women's footwear. It lost its position as a major supplier of shoes only in 1968 when hi-tech competition forced the older factories to close.

Le Mont St Michel

Le Mont St Michel sits in the middle of an enormous area of mud flats and polderland on the borders of Ille et Vilaine and Normandy, joined to the mainland by a causeway. It dominates the eye from all around and, from a distance looks like something out of Disneyland, especially at night when the abbey and the houses below are illuminated by floodlights. It would be hard not to be pleasurably impressed by such a scene.

According to a tenth-century manuscript, the abbey was

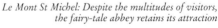

*Le Mont St Michel: Despite the multitudes of visitors,
the fairy-tale abbey retains its attraction*

built in 708 as France and the rest of the old Roman Empire was returning to some semblance of order after the chaos of the Dark Ages. Bishop Aubert of Avaranches, later to be cannonised as St Aubert, was told in a dream to build a shrine on Mont Tombe dedicated to the Archangel Michael, and in recognition of his efforts the church preserved his mortal remains as relics (his skull lies at Avaranches). From this small beginning the shrine prospered and became a centre of homage. Later, the Benedictines founded a monastery and by the end of the tenth century Mont St Michel was famed for its learning and known as the city of books.

Unfortunately, this fame aroused the avarice of King Philippe Auguste, who set fire to the monastery, badly damaging it. To atone for his act of sacrilege the king paid for a new, grander abbey to be built on the hill and, just to be on the safe side, ordered the base of the mount be fortified – indeed the fortifications appear to rise from the very sand in the bay. The result, in spite of a demanding tourist industry, which has turned all but a few of the old buildings in the Grande Rue into shops and restaurants, is one of the wonders of medieval Europe. Houses of all ages and design scramble up the hill and the abbey buildings, including two churches, appear to reach upwards to heaven. Neither the religious significance of the island, nor the substantial fortifications prevented frequent attacks. In the early part of the 15th century the chancel collapsed thanks to its poor construction. However, 600 years later the spire, topped by a gilded effigy of the Archangel Michael, still soars imposingly 525 ft above the waters of the bay.

Rennes

An early Celtic settlement on the top of a hill where the rivers Vilaine and Rance meet, Rennes eventually grew into a major centre for the people of the Redones tribes. It remained important until the Romans under Julius Caesar conquered these fierce but artistic warriors. The town then became an important centre for the Romans.

After the Romans left, Rennes, situated as it is in the centre of the region that was already known as Brittany, was a natural site for the capital. Brittany quickly established a distinctive cultural identity of its own, separate from France and became a

Rennes

Duchy. A parliament was installed in the middle of the 16th century. Throughout its history Brittany experienced a difficult relationship with central government in Paris, and the imposition of a form of stamp duty in the 17th century led to a revolt, with the result that Brittany's parliament was exiled to Vannes from 1675 to 1690 and Rennes occupied by government troops.

One of the most beautiful medieval cities in France, Rennes was full of timber-framed houses and municipal buildings, but in December 1720 a fire broke out that burned for seven days and destroyed or damaged hundreds of buildings. The citizens resolved to rebuild their city as the most modern in France while at the same time incorporating the remaining medieval timber-framed houses and improving and enlarging some of those that had survived the fire.

In the latter part of the 18th century, the king tried to dissolve Brittany's parliament altogether, resulting in riots. According to the writer Chateaubriand, the first blood of the Revolution was spilt in Rennes. The parliament building was very much a symbol of Breton culture. Unfortunately, the stone building, not seriously damaged in the earlier fire, was gutted in 1994; the old timber roof was destroyed as well as, disastrously, much of the Breton archives.

Rennes today is a vibrant city with a busy commercial life. Popular with tourists, it has many superb restaurants and a thriving café culture.

St Malo

St Malo is named after a Welsh monk, St Maclow, who founded a religious community in the sixth century where the suburb of St Servan now stands. The citadel of St Malo itself was built on an island and later reinforced by an encircling stone wall and people from the surrounding countryside sought shelter behind the wall during the many invasions. In quieter times the causeway was built connecting the island to the mainland, a deep-water harbour began to develop and eventually led to St Malo becoming a famous trading port. During the 14th century the citizens declared for the king and St Malo became a separate French province in miniature.

The finest houses were built on the success of the corsairs, pirates with a licence from the king of France to ply their trade. In the 16th century the town's most famous son, Jacques Cartier, sailed across the Atlantic looking for the North-West Passage. He sailed up the St Lawrence River, believing it was the gateway to Asia and when he asked the indigenous tribespeople where he was, they told him the name of their village – which was called 'Canada'. Thinking this was the native name for the entire territory, Cartier so named it and thus discovered what is now one of the largest countries on earth. It is fitting that this wild and beautiful country should be known by a native American name as the ancestors of the people encountered by Cartier had colonised it some eight thousand years before he was born.

During 1944 much of St Malo inside the old city walls (*inter muros*, as it is called) was devastated. However, after the war the citizens decided to rebuild it, stone by stone, as closely resembling the original as possible. The result is remarkable and a credit to their effort and foresight. One of the finest ways to see old St Malo is to walk around the city walls from one of the many gatehouses (*ports*) where you can look down on the maze of streets thronged with visitors and locals. The walk is long, but well worth the effort. Having explored the city from above, you can then choose a café or restaurant in which to take the weight off your feet – or decide which shops to explore. The shopping here is excellent, and not only tourist knick-knacks.

If a long walk is not an option, a tourist 'train' (starting from Port St Vincent) trundles along the streets with a guide pointing out all the places of interest. One of these is the cathedral of St Vincent. Rebuilt from the ruins of the Second World War using much of the original stone, the interior of this marvellous reconstruction is enhanced by brilliant modern stained glass of various shades of blue – from light to dark – giving off an aquamarine tint. Near the main entrance an ancient Celtic style 12th-century font shows that not everything was destroyed in 1944. The acoustics are excellent and recitals and concerts are held throughout the year.

Vitré

Beginning as no more than a series of wooden ramparts surrounding a hill, Vitré grew to be extremely important because of the trade in wool. The town takes its name from a local Gallo-Roman farmer of the third century AD called Vitrius whose estate and imposing villa once stood here. Listed as one of the nine Baronies of Brittany, the castle, a marvel of medieval architecture, was begun in the 11th century and altered and added to up until the 15th century. The 15th century also saw the arrival of the Laval-Vitré family, who moved here after an incursion by the English forced them to flee their castle in Laval.

Both the castle and the town enjoyed a chequered history of prosperity and strife over many centuries, but after the Revolution comparative peace settled on the surrounding countryside.

Today the castle still stands sentinel over the town, the walls a tribute to the stonemasons of a bygone age. Parts of it are open to the public and the muddy moat, remarked upon by Flaubert, has long since drained away. Mown grass now fills the bed of the moat like a green carpet.

Some of the 15th- and 16th-century artisans' shops are still standing and there's a bustling market. It's also a centre for cheese-making and industries involved in beef production, and the associated manufacture of leather shoes.

Morbihan

Beech marten

Introduction

Viewed in abstract, Morbihan sits in the south-west corner of Brittany like a piece of a jigsaw puzzle, its outline indented along the landward side and even more so at the coast with the large estuary of the river Blavet at Lorient, the Rivière d'Etel and, of course, the Golfe du Morbihan – The Little Sea. However, to describe this large, ancient department as merely a piece in a geographic jigsaw would be like describing a Fabergé egg as merely an ornament.

It is a beautiful, fascinating region and holds within its borders some of the most tangible evidence of the early history of our species. Some of the earliest signs of human occupation in Europe can be seen in the shell middens (heaps of discarded oyster and mussel shells) found along the shores of the Golfe du Morbihan, the detritus of hundreds of prehistoric seafood platters eaten by Mesolithic hunter-gatherer peoples, who may well have made spring and autumn pilgrimages to this productive coastline. As family parties of Cro-Magnon Man (the name given by science to the first modern humans, discovered in the Dordogne) scoured the Golfe for shellfish, flocks of birds on a scale we can only imagine, previously isolated from northern Europe for millennia because of the ice sheets, began to return

Brocéliande: One of the most extensive ancient woodlands in Brittany and home to deer, wild boar, pine martens – and the legend of King Arthur

to exploit the thawing landscape and search the developing mud and sand flats for worms and crustaceans.

At the end of the last Ice Age a coastal plain stretched far out beyond the current shoreline. This gently rising land was rich in game and would almost certainly have been colonised by the first humans. As the glaciers melted, however, it gradually became inundated by the rising sea levels that heralded the beginning of a warm period of climatic change between Ice Ages, a period which, incidentally, we are still enjoying today.

The period of the Mesolithic Era to the early Bronze Age, a timescale spanning perhaps 4,000 years, is viewed as if through a misty glass. It's difficult to get a clear view of this period of time because there are so few artefacts to give us clues as to the people and their lifestyle. But later cultures left a more lasting impression on the landscape – as seen in the Breton Celtic names, often prefixed with 'K' or 'Ker', such as small towns and villages like Kernabessec and Kerbodin found not far from St Jean de Brévelay. Near Moustoirac the menhir at Kermarquer is one of only a few remaining standing stones in Brittany that still shows signs of decoration (you can clearly see the crooks carved into it). Several ancient stone monuments are dotted along the granite ridge that is now known as the Landes de Lanvaux, grouped reasonably close together, and certainly close enough to visit most of them in one day. One of the best examples is at Kerguillerme le Moustoir, and further south, near Vannes, the passage graves are extraordinarily numerous.

The most famous megalithic monuments are at Carnac (in the very south of Morbihan) and consist of the Cairn de Kerado, Tumulus Saint-Michel, Tretre du Manio, Dolmen de Kerario and Dolmen de Kerlescan. They are the jewels in the crown of Brittany's prehistory. At Menec, over one thousand stones stand in lines and 70 stones are arranged in an oval among the houses and gardens of the village. It's quite something to see and the visitor centre is excellent, providing a great deal of

Carnac

information about the stones, and platforms from which to view them.

When the Romans invaded this land, creating the Roman province of Armorica, the legions found a well-ordered society ruled by Celtic warlords whose wealth was measured in gold torques and small chariot horses, herds of cattle and flocks of sheep. The Celtic warriors favoured single combat and ambush combined with sheer bravado and they performed astonishing feats of horsemanship and chariot-driving. But neither their style of battle not the hill forts, built as gathering places in times of war, could help them to hold out against the ordered might and war engines of the Roman legions. They were soon routed and the hill forts slighted. The stunningly beautiful 'inland sea' of the Golfe du Morbihan was a stronghold of the western Celtic tribes of the Veneti during the late Iron Age, but a Roman war fleet crushed their resistance in an epic sea battle actually in the Golfe itself. It was one of Rome's very few sea victories.

A period of extreme instability followed the collapse of the Roman Empire until the church began to establish a political and economic power-base. From this time has come a legacy of stories. For instance, the mythological figure of a warrior king called Arthur features as strongly in Breton culture as it does in Britain. It is hard to pin down this person to a particular time and place, if indeed he ever existed at all. However, cut away the mythology and there does appear to have been a shadowy figure, or more probably an amalgam of Romano/Celtic warlords, who held sway either in Gaul or England. The romantics among us should be grateful for the wealth of legend left in 'Arthur's' wake. For example, in the Forêt Domaniale de Paimpont (the ancient, mysterious Brocéliande) these legends abound. The Morbihan Tourist Office has put them to good use, marking out footpaths that lead to sites of historical interest.

Morbihan boasts a wealth of woodlands, with marvellous wildlife-rich examples such as the forest of Lanouée north of

Paimpont: A large lake, beside an ancient abbey where bats hunt insects in the warm evening air

Wild strawberry (Fragaria vesca): *One of the ancestors of domesticated strawberries, the fruit is small, but delicious. Found growing along the banks of sunken lanes and woodland margins*

Josselin, and Camors and Floranges at the northern end of the Landes de Lanvaux. Even this far inland, the sea's influence is apparent, especially on the Landes where pines and oaks, arthritically bent by the prevailing wind, stand guard over acid moors and heathlands intersected by deep wooded valleys. It is a landscape that would be familiar to the people who lived here hundreds, perhaps even thousands, of years ago.

The Morbihan coastline faces the Atlantic Ocean and boasts some fine sandy bays and inlets, the best being found near Lorient, Carnac and Sarzeau. Edged with pale honey-coloured sand and speckled with seashells fragmented by Atlantic gales, beaches backed with marram-grass-topped dunes are juxtaposed with wild and beautiful river valleys that were once the haunt of brigands. It is a well-watered region. When the gigantic European ice sheet began to melt, water poured through the

Séné, Morbihan: A mixture of meadowland, maritime pine woodland and salt marsh full of birds, insects and amphibians. A major wildlife site on the edge of the Golfe du Morbihan

land with enormous force, carving steep valleys in the ancient rocks and carrying boulders and gravel from far inland. Today the waterways have been tamed. In Morbihan several are linked to canals and carry commercial products, although more usually (as in Britain) they are used by pleasure craft.

The rivers Scroff and Blavet (which connects to the Nantes–Brest Canal and the 'Chemin de Halage' that runs from Brest to the Loire) pour their waters into the sea at Lorient, an important fishing port and naval base. The river Loc'h washes the walls of the once defensive historic town of Auray. This river runs into Auray from the north, but when it leaves the town, heading towards the sea through the narrow entrance of the Golfe, its name has changed to the river d'Auray. Auray itself is now a busy tourist and oyster farming centre; it is one of the nine Breton towns awarded the title 'City of Art and History'. Many of Brittany's towns suffered heavy damage during the Hundred Years' War and a great deal of medieval architecture was lost. However, it is some compensation that a lot of towns still parade some delightful 16th- and 17th-century timber-framed houses.

The comparison of this department to a jigsaw puzzle is more than apt considering the astonishing variety and complexity of the countryside and its wildlife inhabitants. From quiet salt marsh to wild high heath, from deep river valleys to fine sandy beaches, there is just about every type of temperate wildlife habitat. There is no doubt that this region has been of importance to humankind through the ages and, fortunately, its best features still remain.

Wildlife

Golfe du Morbihan

Bordered by the towns of Auray and Vannes in the very south of the Morbihan department in southern Brittany, and protected from the Atlantic Ocean by the Presqu'île de Quiberon, the stunningly beautiful Golfe du Morbihan (also called 'La petite mer') constitutes one of the most important sites for passage waders and wildfowl in Western Europe.

The conditions in the Golfe that suit the birds (caused in part by the marine topography) are identical to those that suit the cultivation of mussels and oysters. The sea is forced through the relatively narrow entrance to the Golfe where its power is dissipated. The silt and nutrients fall to the bottom and fertilises a complex pyramidal ecosystem composed of bacteria, algae and seaweeds on which billions of marine worms, shellfish and molluscs feed. In turn these converters of water-borne nutrients feed a host of higher crustaceans from tiny prawns and shrimps to crabs. A visit at high tide to one of the many salt pans or fish farms during the spring or the late summer and early autumn will almost certainly result in sightings of a wide variety of

Damselfly –'the beautiful demoiselle' – (Calopteryx splendens):
A relatively common damselfly of slow-flowing rivers
and deep ponds and lakes

Avocets (Recurvirostra avosetta)*: One of the most attractive wading birds of the salt pans and salt marsh, the high piping calls unmistakeable. (Seen here at Séné)*

passage waders including black and bar-tailed godwits, greenshank, whimbrel, dotterel, golden and grey plover, not to mention the smart little egret, black-winged stilts and avocet, which breed on several nearby reserves.

The way in which nature has adapted certain creatures to thrive on a regime of inundation twice daily is remarkable. In summer the sun bakes the surface of exposed mudflats; winter chills the worms and crustaceans in their deep burrows; and the autumn and spring rains dilute the salts that permeate the marshlands. Nevertheless, these unpromising and hazardous conditions have evolved over time to create a cornucopia for birds and for humankind.

Ten thousand years ago mixed flocks of birds migrated back and forth, from the continent of Africa to Europe, the numbers and variety of species beyond comprehension, although some indication can be drawn from modern-day migration patterns. Millions of wading birds and wildfowl still fly in to the Golfe as the autumn and winter flocks return after a breeding season of long summer days in the high Arctic.

Hunting by wildfowlers exacts a heavy toll on the flocks of waders and duck; even wild swans are not immune. But there are several reserves where hunting is not permitted. The hide on the Marais du Duer reserve near Sarzeau on the Golfe side of the Presqu'île de Rhuys provides excellent views over the mudflats where thousands of Brent geese come in winter to feed. On the Atlantic coast of the peninsula, the marshes at Suscinio and the dunes and marshes at Landrezac-Penvins run together and constitute an enormous (110 hectare) reserve made up of dunes, marshes and reed beds – a marvellous sheltered area for a wide variety of wildlife, including avocet, black-tailed and bar-tailed godwits, flocks of curlew and oystercatchers, and the occasional migrant whimbrel. Autumn and winter are the best time to see grey and purple herons. They fly in from the nearby Brière marshland (on the northern bank of the Loire estuary) at the end of their breeding season, where the grey herons have been breeding in the trees and the purple herons in the reed beds.

Just a few kilometres south of Vannes on a little peninsula that dips into the north-west corner of the Golfe, the Réserve Naturelle des Marais de Séné – Site de Falguéric is based on old salt marshes and salt pans – 220 hectares support an enormous number of passage migrants as well as 48 species of breeding birds including avocet and black-winged stilt. In autumn and winter huge gatherings of knot, sanderling and grey plover, as many as 10,000 to 12,000 birds, regularly fill the air in wreaths of smoke-like clouds as they are driven ahead of the rising tide to roost on the fields and salt pans until the water recedes to expose a treasury of food-rich sediments. Redshank and dunlin exploit different types of food potential in the

Black-winged stilt (Himantopus himantopus)*: One of the most striking waders. In flight the shrill alarm call warns other breeding waders of potential danger*

gutters and mudflats. The longer legs of the redshank allow them to paddle in shallow puddles and catch tiny marine shrimps and soft crabs. Dunlin run to and fro in front of the spume and knot, picking up sand hoppers and minute life forms exposed by the tide. All depend on the ebb and flow of water over sand and mud to bring food to their hungry beaks. The knot take their name from the Danish King Canute (Knut), famous for demonstrating that even an all-powerful medieval king was unable to command the tides.

Despite the enormous influx of human visitors to the Golfe's fine sandy beaches during the holiday months of July and August, this is essentially a quiet, peaceful area and on the sharp undercut dunes that face the sea, sand martin colonies are established in rows like little apartment blocks. These cheerful members of the swallow family seem tolerant of human visitors, though how much pressure they can stand is a moot point.

In common with other parts of Brittany heathland is abundant, formed, in this instance, by naturalised dunes of blown sand that have compacted into acid heath. Nightingales can be heard, even at midday, singing from the depths of a rich hedgerow. Many of the more common hedgerow warblers, particularly blackcaps, can be seen, or more likely heard, in spring. And the exciting white spotted bluethroat breeds in small colonies all along this coastline, usually choosing the earthworks and rocks walls that surround old salt evaporation pans. The male stands with head and reddish tail held high showing off the brilliant blue gorget to any rivals, and sings a scratchy robin-like song from the top of a salt-bleached boulder or weathered fence post. This delightful little bird is vulnerable to change but, fortunately, the profitable practice of fish farming, particularly shellfish farming, on the disused salt pans has ensured the protection of its habitat and survival for the foreseeable future.

The Golfe provides good hunting for birds of prey. Common

buzzards and honey buzzards are commonplace and in summer black kites spin in the thermals looking for carrion. It's also excellent harrier country. All three species – hen harrier, marsh harrier and Montagu's harrier – hunt and breed in the region. Barn owls too are relatively common, as are short-eared owls and little owls.

With its many inlets and quiet, hidden places, the Golfe is perfect for butterflies and moths, with a wide variety of species in spring and summer, including the map butterfly and the European swallowtail butterfly. A considerable acreage of wet meadowland also ensures an ample population of dragonflies and damselflies, with a large number of *libellula* species and the elegant aeshna hawker dragonflies as well as *sympetrum sanguineum* (the red males of this species are usually seen perched on low foliage and on open ground along the pathways.) The demoiselles are the largest damselflies and their strong metallic body colour (blue or green depending on the species) makes them particularly noticeable. The common blue damselfly and

Séné: A mixture of meadow maritime pine woodland and salt marsh full of birds, insects and amphibians

the similar coenagrion species (of which there are eleven in Europe) are quite common over most of northern Europe, and are particularly in evidence around the Golfe.

Brackish pools provide suitable nurseries for spawning marsh frogs and natterjack toads. The 'singing' marsh frogs (if that is the correct expression for their cheerful duck-like quacking) are a feature of Brittany's coastal wetlands. The natterjack toads begin their strident chorus an hour or so before sunset and, when they gather to spawn in sufficient numbers, the noisy chorus can be heard from over a kilometre away.

Since the Stone Age the Golfe du Morbihan has been a treasure-trove, both for humankind and for wildlife. It is still one of the most exciting wildlife refuges in north-western France. Only recently discovered by British birdwatchers, it is beautiful, easily accessible and fascinating: you could spend a whole month here and still not see everything. In an age when wild wetland habitats are in decline it is truly wonderful to find a place like this where a myriad fauna and flora can thrive and prosper in relative safety.

Landes de Lanvaux

North of Vannes, large tracts of sandy heather and gorse-covered heath, interspersed with villages and farmland, stretch almost from Baud in the east to Rochefort en Terre in the west. St Jean de Brévelay

Landes de Lanvaux, Morbihan: An area of heathland and wet moorland full of unique wildlife

Bell heather (Erica cinerea)*: A common plant of
dry heathland found on the Landes of Brittany*

on the D778 is arguably at the centre of the Landes de Lanvaux
– the typical inland Breton heathland, which constitutes a mosaic of habitats for plants, insects, reptiles, mammals and birds.

The common recyclers of nature's detritus, earthworms and
millipedes, cannot survive in acidic heathland soil where organic
matter is in short supply, so the leaf litter dropped by tough
heathers and gorse depends on the action of micro-organisms
to break it down into its component parts. Periodic outbreaks
of fire liberate minerals and nutrients into the impoverished
soil, allowing light and rain to stimulate new growth. Fire also
inhibits the growth of trees that would shade out the heathland
species. In the past grazing animals would have cropped the
plants, reinvigorating the herbage with their droppings, but
now managed fires sustain the heathland and keep it open and

Emperor moth (Saturnia pavonia): *Male. An inhabitant of heath and moorland, often mistaken for a butterfly because of its day-flying character. Found on the Landes of Brittany*

Green hairstreak butterfly (Callophrys rubi): *An early spring butterfly of heathland and woodland margins, the upper wing is dark brown providing excellent camouflage against a hedgerow*

productive for wildlife, controlling insects like the heather beetle which will strip the foliage from heather in high infestation years. This specialised habitat often supports 25 or more species of heathland beetles. Carnivores belong to the family of carabids (ground beetles.) Among the more interesting members of this family are the tiger beetle larvae, adapted to trap ants and used as unwitting models for science fiction horror movies. The larvae live at the base of steep-sided, funnel-shaped depressions, which they dig in the dry sandy soil. There they sit, pincer-shaped mandibles hidden in the loose sand. When an ant or other similar-sized ground-living insect stumbles in, the sand slip carries it inexorably into the jaws of the larvae. There are oil beetles, dung beetles and minotaur beetles, which act as janitors, clearing up droppings; and leaf beetles and heather beetles, which provide food for the larger animals.

For all their outward appearance of sterility, heathlands are home to an astonishing variety of moths, from tiny fly-like micro-lepidoptera to the large and beautiful emperor moth. The butterflies here are less abundant but, like many denizens of the heather, are unique to this habitat. The grayling butterfly thrives here – a member of the worldwide order of 'Browns' it is superbly camouflaged in grey and brown and gold with life-like eyespots to confuse birds into attacking this part of the wing rather than the soft vulnerable body. Another speciality of heathland is the exquisite silver-studded blue butterfly; the name derives from the silver markings on the under wing whereas the upper wing is bright blue, edged with lunules of red and black with a white fringe. In April and May the visually elusive green hairstreak butterfly hatches as a perfect insect, but so tiny, it would fit neatly on a Euro coin. The underwing is a brilliant, slightly reflective green and the upper wing a sombre shade of sepia. It is so well camouflaged that, when it flies, it almost vanishes against the green-brown foliage of the gorse, one of its larval food plants. Like many of the hairstreak and blue butterflies, the green hairstreak further adds to its camouflage capabilities by lying flat on a leaf when it is resting.

In April and May adders, smooth snakes and sand lizards wake from hibernation. The milder climate also encourages other reptiles, such as green lizards (which have a limited range and population in Great Britain.) The lizards stalk the spiders – as do spider-hunting wasps – and the lizards themselves are preyed on by birds, smooth snakes, adders, toads and other, larger green lizards.

Although heaths are basically dry, they often hold large areas of standing water, particularly where an impervious fold in the

Below: *Adder or common viper* (Vipera berus)*:*
Although poisonous, adders have an undeserved reputation.
They are shy and would rather escape than attack
Opposite: *Toads* (Bufo bufo)*: Long-lived and well*
protected by poison glands, the common toad is
very much a creature of dry heathland

land allows a pond, small lake, or a valley bog to develop. As well as providing for mammals and birds to drink and to bathe, the water is an oasis for amphibians, particularly heathland-adapted species like the palmate newt and natterjack toad and for insects like damselflies and dragonflies. Because the soil is low in nitrogen and the water acidic, all heathland ponds are destined in the longer term to fill with peaty plant remains. The highly specialised plants that grow in these tea-coloured ponds are limited, but fascinating nonetheless, and flowering plants such as bog bean are superbly adapted. The plants that grow on the swampy margins, such as common sundew, supplement their meagre diet with a fly or two, captured on sticky mobile leaves that enfold and digest the unfortunate insect. Marsh gentian, pale butterwort and heath spotted orchid make a living where there is moisture and the processes of plant decay sufficiently advanced for them to extract the nutrients they need.

Pools of standing water produce a wide variety of dragonflies and the returning hobby falcons are not slow to show their aerial prowess by chasing and catching these most manoeuvreable of insects with consummate ease.

In winter, heathland can be quiet. There is little birdsong and perhaps only a buzzard circling lazily seeking rabbits or carrion. This is a closed cycle habitat needing the spring and summer sun to bring it to life, and rain. Rainwater washes the nutrients out of the topsoil but, paradoxically, heathland is, for the most part, free draining, and therefore almost a desert environment where only those plants and animals specially adapted to dry conditions can prosper. And this, in large measure, is its attraction for naturalists.

Generally speaking heathland has a poor public image, a reputation that observation will soon refute. From April onwards it begins to stir, and with the warming sun come the first of the spring migrant birds – warblers, chats and flycatchers on passage. Stonechats tuck themselves in along the heathland margins and the beautiful male sings from the very tips of the low growing heather, while whinchats are very much at home on the open heath and sing their simple song from the top of the gorse bushes. Male wheatears flirt their tails and rush from ant hill to ant hill to attract the attention of passing females; later they seek out disused rabbit burrows in which to build a nest.

Heathland is a vital habitat for several birds, particularly the nightjar, Dartford warbler and hobby. As the sun goes down so the nightjar begins its nightly harvesting of moths. They fly as if on invisible wires, floating over the gorse, often following pathways. The males, easily distinguished from the astonishingly camouflaged females by their white wing spots, unusually sit sideways along a branch rather than across it as they churr their love songs. In Britain, the Dartford warbler (*fauvette pitchou* in France) is at the northern limit of its range. Happily it is relatively common on the Breton heathlands where the plum-coloured males snatch a scatter of song from the tips of the heather or gorse before disappearing back into the dense under scrub. They breed close to the ground and are superb at camouflaging their nests.

The saying goes: 'Love will never die while the gorse blooms.' In the mild Breton climate, there are always a few brilliant yellow gorse flowers on show – all through the year. But it is in the early spring that this prickly plant begins the most extravagant flower show, one that will last right through until October.

Forêt Domaniale de Paimpont (Brocéliande)

With Rennes to the east, St Méen to the north and Ploërmel to the south-west, the forest of Paimpont can be reached either from the D766, or perhaps more easily from the N24. At Campénéac pick up the D332 which turns into the D40: this scenic route leads straight to the town of Paimpont, an excellent centre from which to explore the whole area.

Three departments meet here – Morbihan, Ille et Vilaine and Côtes d'Amor – in the region known as Paimpont ('penpon' means bridge-head in Breton). Bordered by the river Meu to the east and the river Oust to the west, and touched on its southern flank by the river Aff, this well-watered area has been covered with broadleaved woodland since the end of the last Ice Age. Once inhabited by the Druids, the legendary forest of Brocéliande is closely connected with many events in the tales of King Arthur and the Knights of the Round Table. Today, the 18,000 acres that remain are merely a remnant of the vast primeval forest that once stretched from Rennes to Rostrenen. But a network of paths lead to many of the ancient stone monuments, some of which are 6,000 years old; they were built by the shadowy late Stone Age/early Bronze Age pastoral society that once inhabited the region. These stones, mostly built on rising ground, indicate a deeply spiritual society, and have

Brocéliande: Etang du Pas du Houx. In the heart of the forest of Brocéliande the marshes and reedbeds around the old hammer ponds provide breeding grounds for millions of common toads. The hammerponds themselves once provided the head of water to drive the mill wheels and trip hammers for iron working

Fallow deer (Cervus dama): A medium sized deer and a member of the fauna of Europe since the last Ice Age. Now maintained as an animal of the hunt and as an ornamental species in parks

been incorporated into the Arthurian legend (Viviane's House, Merlin's Tomb and the Fountain of Youth).

The whole area is as rich in wildlife as it is in historic relics and legendary tales. The underlying ancient rock is composed of schist and limestone, metamorphosed by the volcanic action that threw up the original dark mountains of Brittany. Time and the elements have worn down the hills, and their constituent minerals have leached into rivers once panned for gold and silver by the Celts. The soil is poor and encourages the growth of woodland, much of which is privately owned and managed for hunting.

Whatever your reaction to hunting and field sports, there is little doubt that pheasant shooting and stalking deer and wild boar have protected this landscape, which would almost certainly have been ploughed for crops or converted to conifer plantations had it not been for its value as a hunting preserve. It is to be hoped that in the future better environmental education and the growing strength of organisations like the LPO (Ligue pour la Protection des Oiseaux) and an increase in eco-tourism will change attitudes towards the quite remarkable wildlife

Wild boar (Sus scrofa)*: The ancestor of all European domesticated pigs, these shy creatures have a reputation for bravery*

heritage of France.

Spring is perhaps the most exciting time of year, with the pale flowers of butterfly orchids hiding in the shade of the trees and carpets of common spotted orchids, many of them a pure white subspecies, growing along the roadside verges and forest rides. Wild flowers are a speciality of many French woodlands, but the size and ancient nature of this particular woodland creates just the right conditions to support a large number of orchid species. Early marsh orchids bloom in the wetter areas and, where layers of limestone lie close to the surface, lady orchids and early purple orchids thrive. Acid-loving plants such as sundews thrive here too, especially on the hillsides – as does Dorset heath, a moorland plant – and mats of biting stonecrop cover the rocks around some of the monuments.

Between late April and September the woodland and open heathland are alive with butterflies. Ancient forest encourages rare species like the purple emperor, white admiral and pearl-bordered and small pearl-bordered fritillary butterflies, and the European swallowtail butterfly is relatively common in high summer, as are the map butterfly and the speckled wood butterfly. Around the lakes and streams and along the damp margins of the woodland the marsh fritillary butterfly can be seen in some numbers, while the heath fritillary butterfly occurs in the marginal area between the woodland and the heath.

Lesser butterfly orchid (Platanthera bifolia): *A woodland plant, this pale beauty is fertilised by hawkmoths*

It pays to be observant in old woodland – especially here. Brocéliande contains one of the most important hunting preserves in France for wild boar, a creature rarely seen, and then perhaps only a fleeting glimpse by chance between the trees. Large, dark in colour and medieval-looking, the wild boar is now surrounded by a great deal of mythology, especially in respect to its fierce nature and the way in which it is supposed to attack without provocation. The ancestor of all Europe's domesticated

Early purple orchid (Orchis mascula): *Grows along woodland rides in company with stitchwort and bluebells. Once thought to be an aphrodisiac because of the double tubers, but this has no basis in fact. Thrives in the forests at Brocéliande*

pigs, the wild boar is renowned for its intelligence and ability to sense danger. Exceptionally good hearing and sense of smell makes it extremely difficult to get close to a wild boar, unless conditions are exactly right; and its eyesight, though far from perfect, is more than adequate to detect movement in their forest environment. It is the natural desire of wild boar to avoid humankind – with very good reason.

Spring is when the sows give birth. The piglets, usually about ten in a litter, are striped with black and yellow and blend into the light and shade dapple of the springtime forest floor. Mortality among the piglets is high due to road casualties and a certain amount of predation by foxes and domestic dogs. In the 14th and 15th centuries the European wolves inhabiting these forests would have been the prime predator of the young wild boar.

The creation of the ecosystem here owes much to the efforts of hundreds of generations of wild boar and of deer. The boars turn the soil as they hunt for food, creating just the right conditions for the seeds of wild plants and trees to germinate and the deer control the growth of tree saplings by constantly browsing, and by fraying the trunks in autumn during the rut.

Two species of deer inhabit the woodlands: fallow deer, the traditional deer of the chase with flattened palmate antlers with tines of sharp bone around the edge of the flat plate of bone; and the smaller species, roe deer. About the size of a large dog and dark brown in colour, roe deer sport a pair of sharp antlers with one or more tines growing from a central spike. The boar and the deer are at the top of the mammalian population, but small mammals thrive here too, especially red squirrels which leave stripped pinecones littered about after feasting on the seeds. The squirrels are preyed on by pine martens and to a lesser extent beech martens, though the latter are more usually found near farms where they thrive on rats and mice.

One of the most fascinating aspects of established woodland

Roe deer buck

is the presence of large areas of standing water. There are several lakes here, some of which are man-made, others are natural and have been enhanced and enlarged.

Attached to the abbey at Paimpont is a large lake that supports a variety of wildlife species both in and above the water. The abundant insect life encourages swifts, which breed in the roof of the old abbey building and in the chapel. The scores of swallows and house martins that nest all around the village join in the harvest of the hatching midges. As evening draws in the night shift of bats and owls takes over. Huge numbers of Daubenton's, long-eared and Natterer's bats, as well as the little pipistrelle bats, pour out from their day-time roosts in the abbey and in the many old houses, barns and farm buildings nearby to feed over the lake.

Much of this area is privately owned and part of large country estates. One such estate borders the Etang du Pas du Houx, a large natural lake with an enormous population of amphibians. In spring and early summer the grass around the margins of the lake and the reed beds is alive with frogs and toads. The croaking of the pool frogs and edible frogs can be heard from some considerable distance. With this much food about, naturally, the heron population is high, but the areas where they breed are not open to the public.

The number and species of birds of prey is also high over the whole forest. Honey buzzards are relatively common and breed in the woodlands, as do black kites, common buzzards, sparrow-hawks, kestrels and goshawks. The outer margins of the wooded areas and the farmland support breeding pairs of Montagu's harriers and marsh harriers.

The small bird population in spring is substantial, as befits woodland of this size and variety. You might even hear a black woodpecker calling in the mature conifers plantations. Green, grey-headed, lesser-spotted, greater-spotted and middle-spotted woodpeckers can also be seen – although more likely to be heard drumming in April and early May. Songbirds, including blackbirds, song thrushes, golden oriole and a host of migrant warblers join together to create the most marvellous dawn chorus.

What you see and hear will depend on how much time you have at your disposal to walk quietly through the dappled light filtering down through the forest of Brocéliande.

Towns and Villages

Auray

This pretty town makes its living from the increasing numbers of tourists that flock here in summer, and from the productive oyster fishery based on the estuary of the river Loc'h. The patrician houses in the town centre and in the port area date from the 16th century and the equally fine Hôtel Dieu dates from the middle of the 17th century; the whole area has been designated a 'City of Art and History'. During this era the port was the third largest in Brittany, trading in everything from whale oil to corn and salt cod. The port area itself, St Goustan, is on the other side of the river from the town centre reached by an arched bridge. Originally people crossed the river over a ford at low tide, or ferry at high tide, and a bridge was not built until the 13th century. Unfortunately it wasn't strong enough to withstand the tides and was rebuilt and strengthened in the 14th century, using the original piers.

The spiritual side of Auray was fundamental to its importance. In 1623 Yves Nicolazic had a series of visions of a lady in white and a message led him to uncover a painted statue in a nearby field. This 'miracle' so enthralled the townspeople and members of the church that a shrine was built, dedicated to St Anne, the Virgin's Mother. It's still a religiously important place with pilgrimages and 'Pardons' taking place from Easter until October.

A costume museum was opened in 1920 with a large display of traditional Breton costumes. There is also a Folk Art gallery with around about 100 statues carved and painted by local craftsmen between the 15th and 19th centuries.

Lorient

Founded on the mouth of the river Blavet in the mid-17th century by Louis XIV to capitalise on the spice trade between France and the East Indies, the port grew rapidly as a ship-building centre. One of the first merchantmen built for the Compangnie des Indes was the 1,000-tonne Soleil d'Orient that became known as L'Orient – a short step to Lorient. The trade in silks from China and goods and spices to and fro the Spice Islands prospered until the French lost their major trading routes as a result of the War of Spanish Succession. A new company was formed to trade in the Americas, the West Indies, and Africa and again in the China markets for silks, tea, spices and porcelain, but its success was short-lived and the town became what it is today: a naval shipyard and ship-building centre with an expanding fishing fleet that now serves the Parisian market.

During the Second World War Lorient was a base for U-Boats, and by 1945 most of the old town had been destroyed by bombing, although in the Merville district, some fine examples of art nouveau and art deco houses remain, as does the fine War Memorial. Of course, the massive stone and reinforced concrete submarine pens survived too and now house the French Navy's nuclear submarines.

Lorient is a fascinating town with many interesting aspects. The annual Inter-Celtic Festival of Dance, Songs and Art from the Celtic world of Brittany, Cornwall, Wales, Scotland, Ireland and northern Spain (the region known as Galicia) takes place here in August and attracts large numbers.

There's a sailing marina, tripper boats that run to the Golfe du Morbihan, and a ferry runs between the Boulevard Auguste Pierre (near the Maison de la Mer) and the island of Groix, about 45 minutes away. There's an excellent signposted coastal path all around the island (5 miles long by 2.5 miles wide), which has been a tuna-fishing centre since the 14th century; no doubt the inhabitants were fishing the Gulf Stream long before then. The Eco Museum provides a snapshot of the islands' prehistory, geology and wildlife. Perfectly situated on the north-south migration flight lines, the Ile de Groix is renowned for rare migrant birds from all over Northern Europe and the cliffs hold seabird colonies with large numbers of guillemots, razorbills, kittiwakes and shags.

Paimpont

Paimpont owes its existence to the abbey, which dominates the lake. After the Romans left Gaul, law and order collapsed and the church struggled to fill the power vacuum that developed. Judicael, a royal prince who became a monk, founded a hermitage here, which evolved into a monastery in the 12th century. Judicael duly became King of Domnone in Brittany and famously defended his kingdom against the incursions of the Franks before retiring back to his monastic life.

The town is surrounded by forest, a remnant of the legendary Brocéliande that once stretched in an unbroken swathe across southern Brittany. The Basse Forêt to the east and the Haute Forêt to the west consist of lovely thick woodland interspersed with heathland and peat bog, lakes and streams. The local geology is rich in ironstone and outcrops of metamorphosed limestone. The availability of so much wood for charcoal and lakes and streams to provide power made it a natural iron-working site, and the forge at d'en Bas has recently been restored.

Quimper

The old city of Quimper sits on the banks of the river Odet, about 18 kilometres from the sea. An interesting historical perspective can be found in the fact that the original Celtic inhabitants may have been witness to the rise in sea level as the continental ice sheets lost their grip in the warming climate. Legend has it that the original city was closer to the sea. Called Ys, it was the refuge of King Gradlon who fled from Britain bringing with him the name Cornouaille. His daughter was notoriously difficult and is said to have drowned when the rising water consigned Ys to the bottom of the sea.

Celtic and Roman remains have long disappeared. Undoubtedly much of the Roman masonry was recycled and used in the ramparts erected at the beginning of the 13th century by the Duke of Brittany who was also Conte de Cornouaille. He had the city enclosed within sturdy walls supported by ten towers and six fortified gates. The 13th century saw the flowering of the cathedral building movement in France, and St Corentin, with its offset alignments of choir and nave is an excellent example. Impressive stone spires were added in 1856, paid for by a levy on each and every parishioner.

The former Bishop's Palace houses the Brittany Museum, with a collection of traditional furniture and the distinctive local pottery for which the town is famous. Jean Baptist Bousquet, a potter from Provence, opened a workshop in the 15th century, which is still producing pottery today called HB. The designs range from the art deco style to the famous teardrop-shaped brush strokes of the decoration called 'du Petit Breton' – featuring a peasant in traditional costume of blue jacket and pantaloons standing between two designs of vegetation.

Only a few of the original timber and cob houses remain following a fire in the 16th century that destroyed much of the old quarter around the cathedral. As a consequence, building in the old style was forbidden and the timber-framed buildings were replaced by stone, although the medieval atmosphere remains, particularly in the old quarter. As the city developed so the river Odet, which runs to the sea through impressive rock encrusted valleys, was canalised. The old banks were built over, but the river retains its nautical flavour, particularly as the water that runs far inland is largely salt and not heavily influenced by the fresh water from inland.

La Roche Bernard

Thought to owe its foundation to Viking settlers who, on discovering this beautiful harbour in a tidal estuary surrounded by forests, began the boat building industry that supported the town for centuries. It was particularly prosperous after the promulgation of the Edict of Nantes in 1598, when religious toleration meant that craftsmen of different denominations were able to work together for the benefit of all. The keels of several large wooden warships were laid down in the shipyards during the 17th and early 18th centuries, and shipbuilding ran hand in hand with the construction of the stout wood-framed and planked grain-carrying vessels that plied the river Vilaine to the enrichment of the corn merchants and the farming community. Later the chaos and confusion of the French Revolution and the subsequent Chouan uprising drained away both the population and the prosperity. There is a record of a guillotine being set up in the old town square.

Designated a 'City of Character', La Roche Bernard is indeed an attractive town. The old quarter, Place du Buffay, is a fine place to sit and enjoy a coffee, an aperitif or a meal and watch the world go by. Lying in the valley of the river Vilaine, which is itself dominated by a splendid modern suspension bridge, the town basks in quiet contemplation of its modern role as a prime tourist centre for sailing and boardsailing, pleasure boats and river cruising.

Redon

A spring or summer visit to this pretty river port is one of flowery splendour. Tourists are greeted with a profusion of flowers: houses are bedecked with window boxes and hanging baskets. Redon has worked hard to create this impression and has justly earned the title 'Ville Fleurie', 'town of flowers'.

Situated in a strategic position at the conjunction of the rivers Vilaine and Oust, it was an important crossing place for centuries. During the 18th century the river trade (Redon acted as a seaport for Rennes) brought even greater prosperity and the old town centre bears witness to the wealth of the merchants who built their wood-framed and corbelled houses within sight of the river and the quay. Then as part of his design for strategic waterways throughout France, Napoleon decreed that the converging rivers should be joined to create the Nantes–Brest Canal. The canal crosses the town with a complex of locks that will delight students of hydraulics and possibly overawe the many pleasure boaters that ply the waterways during the holiday season.

The area around Redon has been inhabited for at least 3,000 years. Indeed if the large numbers of stone menhir, alignments and tombs to be found to the north of the town near the village of St Just, in the region known as the Landes de Cojoux, are anything to go by, pre-Celtic tribes farmed the land and kept sheep and cattle on the fertile grassland and in the forests as far back as 5,000 years ago. Before the Romans, this region was the territory of a powerful Celtic tribe called the Redones and, despite the fact that the ruling chieftains were overrun by Caesar's legions, the town kept its original name. The Romans created a trading centre here using the two rivers to supply the region under their control. When the Roman Empire collapsed and the legions devolved back to Rome, Redon continued as a trading port and a market town for agricultural produce from the surrounding countryside, including chestnuts. They are still grown today, and Redon holds a festival and a famous Chestnut Market at the end of October.

Redon has adapted well to the modern age. Computers and clothes have been added to the local industry. It is still a distribution centre for agriculture, and a popular tourist centre based on river cruising. It's an extremely pleasant place to spend a day or two, exploring the local countryside, enjoying the food and, of course, the flowers.

Rochefort en Terre

Sitting on an outcrop of hard granitic rock and schist high above the valley of the river Gueuzon, a tributary of the river Arz, Rochfort en Terre lies at the eastern end of the Landes de Lanvaux and has been associated with humankind since the Palaeolithic period. The name comes from the family Rochfort who built a castle in the 12th century in defence of the road from Malestroit to La Roche Bernard but, after a chequered history, the 18th-century version was dismantled. This is one of the prettiest towns in Brittany; many of the buildings have been restored, and even television aerials have to be concealed and electric cables buried. Most of the streets are cobbled and there are some rather beautiful 16th - and 17th-century houses.

The 12th-century church, Notre Dame de la Tronchaye, boasts a carved gallery created with the woodwork from an ancient rood screen. The Calvary, outside the church, is early 16th century and was used as a visual aid to teach poor people the Catechism.

Vannes

Vannes owes its name to the Breton word 'Gwenea', which means 'The Place of the Veneti.' This important tribe of Celts constructed their hilltop settlements beside the Golfe du Morbihan and made the area their headquarters. However Julius Caesar defeated the Veneti in a classic sea battle in the Golfe itself, and afterwards developed the settlements into a major trading post, which it continued to be, even through the difficult period of the Hundred Years' War. Much later in its history, a union between Brittany and France in the 16th century ended much of the almost continuous strife, and Vannes developed into one of the most important cities in the former Duchy. To add to its importance the Breton parliament was moved from Rennes to Vannes, though this parliament is long since dissolved.

The archaeological museum at the Château Gaillard houses a major display of objects and artefacts found in the Golfe du Morbihan, ranging from Neolithic and Bronze Age jewellery to Iron Age weapons and pottery and Gallo-Roman pottery and coins. In recent times the strategic importance of Vannes has been limited and during the Second World War it was spared severe damage. In consequence much of the architectural heritage has been preserved, including the half-timbered houses in Place Henri IV and Rue St Gwenaë, and the medieval house at no. 3 Rue Bienfaisance, which is one of the finest in the city.

The 15th-century cathedral of St Pierre boasts a high vaulted nave surrounded by chapels. One of these, the chapel of the Holy Sacrament, is a masterpiece in the Italian Renaissance style. Opposite the cathedral is an unusual building known as the Cohue. It is one of the oldest buildings in Vannes and has been used in turn as a market, courthouse, theatre and even the home of the Breton Parliament. Now it houses the Musée des Beaux Arts.

Foods of the Region

In essence the cuisine of Brittany is based on produce from the sea, the Armor. An enormously long coastline, combined with an abundance of deep sheltered inlets and clean waters, provides a series of ideal breeding grounds for naturally occurring shellfish. That shellfish have been a significant food source for humankind over the millennia is an undisputed fact. The huge Neolithic shell middens of mussel, oyster and clam shells found in Brittany show clearly that Cro-Magnon Man was as fond of a seafood platter as his modern-day counterpart.

Products of the sea have also been used to benefit the land. Seaweed and mud from the many estuaries was once used to make the acidic, sandy inland soil more fertile, and today over a million Bretons are still actively engaged in farming. Apples and sheep, in equal measure, are as fundamental to the region's cuisine as the seafood.

It is thought that the culinary apple developed about 3,000 to 4,000 years ago from a naturally occurring sport of the crab apple (*Malus sylvestris*). From these hard, acidic, but good-keeping fruits, an entire industry of fruit-farming and cider-making has developed. The pear too had a similar, though later development, from the wild species (*Pyrus communis*) into an ingredient for delicious desserts, or fermented with a variety of other fruit juices and sweeteners to create what in English is called Perry and what the French call *Poiré*.

Economic stability, through the availability of a regular food source, enabled people to build monuments like those at Carnac. This stability was based on pigmeat. Our ancestors developed the wild boar into a breed of domesticated pig. These pigs foraged in the surrounding woodlands and quickly grew to maturity. They produced large litters which, in turn, meant that a large number of people were able to congregate in one place over a longer period of time and be fed by means of this readily available high protein food. Previously the hunter-gatherer peoples had had to roam up and down the countryside following and hunting the herds of wild animals.

However, it was sheep, rather than pigs, that represented the wealth of the community. The same is true today in the region around the Baie du Mont St Michel where a particular breed of sheep, the *Pré Salé*, have adapted to the highly salt-contaminated grassland and feed on this enormous floodplain in their thousands. Sheep prospered on the poor grazing of the salt marshes and also on the acidic Landes and high ground of central Brittany. Proof, if proof is needed, of both this wealth and stability can be seen in the numerous villages, built on prehistoric settlements and occupying the same site for several thousands of years.

Oysters and Mussels (Cancale and the Baie du Mont St Michel)

Reading the manifests of Roman military leaders and copies of Roman cookbooks, it is clear that shellfish were an important part in the diet of the all-conquering legions. Brittany's huge natural beds of oysters, mussels and clams must have provided easy provisioning for the shellfish-loving cohorts.

The natural beds are no longer raked and dredged. It is not an exploitative industry today now that science has lent a hand. The shellfish are grown and protected from predators and excessive overfishing by aquaculture specialists; thousands of tonnes of shellfish are produced for the insatiable demands of French gourmands and, of course, visitors.

After they hatch, oysters, mussels and clams spend part of their life as free-swimming creatures before building layers of calcium-rich shell to protect their vulnerable soft bodies.

Oysters and mussels lend themselves to farming on an industrial scale. In the case of oysters, pieces of oyster shell are put out into redundant salt-making ponds to provide an anchor for the tiny shellfish, which are cared for until they reach about 3 to 4 cm (1½ inches) then put out to grow on specially constructed platforms in the sea. The growth of oysters is measured by the amount of shell they lay down. Some species are flat, whereas others have the typical rough 'claw shape' of a natural oyster. They are harvested at various stages in their life cycle to provide oysters for the table that vary in size (and therefore price) from medium to very large.

Cancale is the place to see and eat oysters. At low tide the oyster beds are exposed and stretch across the mud as far as the eye can see. The Museum of Oysters, on the Aurore beach, along the coast road into Cancale from St Benoit des Ondes, is open everyday from mid February to mid September. It furnishes everything there is to know about oyster farming, and tasting too.

Vivier sur Mer, on the coast road from Mont St Michel to Cancale, is the region's centre of mytiliculture (mussel farming), producing about 10,000 tonnes each year; and the Golfe du Morbihan, in southern Brittany, also boasts a good production of mussels. In the Baie du Mont St Michel 20 kilometres of mussel beds are based on posts and frames. The seed mussels are anchored in their millions in sacks attached to wooden posts, or to ropes wound round these posts, and left to grow until they are of marketable size. It's possible to visit these mussel beds and get a closer look: an unusual amphibious craft takes people on guided tours over the muddy sand.

Clams are also seeded into estuaries and along muddy fore-shores and are harvested when mature. These bivalves live in the mud and sandy silt found in estuaries and in shallow sea water. Filter feeders like mussels and oysters take their own share of the microscopic bounty of the fertile sea that washes the Brittany coast. Other shellfish, such as winkles and whelks occur naturally and are harvested from the seashore all around the coast.

The life cycle of oysters, mussels and clams has been studied intensively so that now every stage can be controlled, and, it must be said that shellfish farming has been a factor in the reduction of gastric upsets that can arise from eating naturally occurring shellfish. The knowledge gained by farming shellfish has helped to keep the coastline and estuaries relatively un-polluted in the interests of gastronomy.

Oysters are most adaptable. Eat them raw with a squeeze of lemon and a little pepper or add them to a *cassoulet de poisson* where they complement the flavours of the other fish. Mussels too are used in a variety of fish dishes, where they add a subtle texture and flavour. However, they are best known as *Moules Marinières* (see recipe opposite), one of France's most famous exports. An old peasant recipe, this dish was the staple of coastal villages in hard times, providing much needed protein.

Fruits de Mer are a gastronomic delight. Everything is encased in a stone jacket and amazingly difficult to get at. It's fun though. If only you could wear a Sou'wester or a wet suit!

Produce from the land

The region's proximity to the Atlantic ensures a relatively frost-free environment, just the right conditions for a wide variety of fruit and vegetables. Much of the produce found in the local

Moules Marinières

Mussels must be thoroughly cleaned and bearded
1. Wash the mussels thoroughly under cold running water
2. Scrape each one free of barnacles and seaweed
3. Remove the fibrous beard which protrudes between the shells
4. Don't use cracked or open mussels

<u>Serves 6</u>

5lb (2kg) mussels	Small bunch parsley
Ground black pepper	2 pints (1 litre) Muscadet
8 cloves garlic	1 bouquet garni
2 shallots	2 oz butter

Put the cleaned mussels in a large saucepan. Add pepper to taste. Then add the chopped garlic, shallots and parsley. Pour in the Muscadet and add the bouquet garni. Cover and cook over a high heat for 8 minutes. Shake well to ensure that all the mussels have opened. Add the butter and cook for another 5 minutes. Remove the bouquet garni and serve immediately – with the juice.

markets comes from small organic family farms, some of which also produce goat's and sheep's milk cheeses and honey, and often sell their wares at the farm gate.

Brittany Ferries, one of the companies that now ply the Channel carrying huge numbers of tourists, had their beginnings in Brittany's beleaguered agriculture. The ships were originally commissioned to move the region's superb fruit and vegetable crops, particularly cauliflowers and artichokes, to new markets in Britain. Brittany Ferries still carry fruit and vegetables as well as their human cargo – an interesting combination of two industries.

Cider from Brittany

There is a notional line, drawn between the river Loire (with an e) where it reaches the sea west of Nantes, and the River Loir (without an e) near Angers. Above this line is the fiefdom of king apple and queen pear and below is the province of the grape.

Having been brought up in Devon and Cornwall, we're good judges of quality cider. The ready availability of large numbers of apples in Brittany, particularly in the areas around Fouesnant and Rance Valley (indeed throughout this part of France) with its multitude of orchards, means there is plenty of raw material for producing this refreshing alcoholic drink. The best cider is made by using a variety of mainly non-eating apples, most of them red or yellow, small and hard with varying levels of acidity. And it takes a cider-maker of talent to bring the best out in them. Cider bought at the farm gate is variable, but if you're lucky it can be some of the very best.

Perry, crafted from pears, is made in the same way as apple cider. Indeed pears are sometimes added to the blend of apples that make up the cider juice prior to fermentation. It gives a slightly different style and flavour. The length of fermentation defines whether the finished product will be sweet or dry – and this applies both to perry and cider. A short ferment will mean high sugar content (sweet cider or *cidre doux*). A long ferment will produce a dry cider with a higher alcohol content (dry cider or *cidre brut*).

Calvados

Not all the apples are pressed and fermented directly into cider. In the north of the region, *Calvados*, a powerful spirit (more often associated with Normandy) is distilled from the fermented apple juice – and comes into its own after a long life in a cask or bottle, often in excess of ten years. The flavour lends itself well in cooking, especially pork dishes and, of course, apple puddings.

Pommeau

An apple-based aperitif, rather like an apple port, *Pommeau* is a natural development of cider and perry-making. Mixed with *Calvados* or *Eau de Vie*, it is then matured in oak casks. A good *Pommeau* should be at least three years old and between 16% and 18% alcohol.

Eau de Vie

A potent, sometimes colourless spirit distilled from the production of a single apple type, the small, hard, yellow fruit of Damelot apples. This fruit ripens in mid winter and is pressed, fermented and distilled. *Eau de Vie* takes few prisoners, but encourages many converts.

Other Specialities: Galettes, Crêpes, Far Breton Pudding and Biscuits

The *Breton Galette*, a sort of pancake made with buckwheat flour, was once the staple food for peasants in Brittany who used to eat them with sardines. These days it's usually ham and eggs. Crêpes are made with wheat flour and, generally, filled with sweet things – caramelised apple with Calvados being one of many extremely tasty examples. Another speciality of the region is *Far Breton*, a rich solid flan made with rum, prunes and vanilla. Often served just on its own, it does benefit from a little cream poured over it, or a scoop of vanilla ice cream.

Brittany specialises in several different sorts of 'very moreish' biscuits. The best known are the butter shortbreads *Traou Mad Galettes de Pont Aven*, and *Playben Galettes* (don't confuse them with buckwheat *galettes*), and *Crêpes Dentelles* – mouthwatering concoctions of paper thin biscuit, folded over and over – sometimes plain, sometimes coated in chocolate and flavoured with orange.

Recommended

North Brittany

Hôtel France & Chateaubriand, St Malo (Hotel & Restaurant) Excellent position, just inside the walls of the old city near the St Vincent Gate, fronted by a large square and several cafés and restaurants. The hotel's own restaurant is good too. Garaging available, which is extremely useful as parking is difficult in the narrow streets of the *inter muros*. English spoken.

Pomme d'Or, St Malo (Restaurant) Situated just inside the Grande Porte (to the left), this traditional French hotel exudes a warm Gallic atmosphere and serves excellent food.

Querrien – Cancale (Restaurant only) One of the 30 or more restaurants that line the sea front at Cancale. Attractive interior decoration reminiscent of a ship. Superb seafood and excellent service.

Southern Brittany

Hôtel Armoric, Bénodet (Hotel & Restaurant) Family run hotel with a warm, friendly atmosphere. Private parking facilities, comfortable, pleasantly furnished bedrooms, swimming pool, lovely large garden with tables and chairs, all add to the benefits of this hotel, which makes a marvellous base for exploring southern Brittany. Dinner in the hotel's own restaurant is available if required. The menu changes daily and is displayed in the foyer (or by request). The food is excellent – don't forget to book in. English, Dutch & German spoken.

The nearby Ile Tudy has a couple of good restaurants worth trying.

Sainte Marine (Hotel & Restaurant) Right on the quay of this peaceful little port on the opposite bank of the Odet to Bénodet, this pretty small hotel has nine comfortable rooms. The restaurant, decorated in the colours of the sea, serves wonderful local dishes.

Central Brittany

Hôtel Relais de Brocéliande (Hotel & Restaurant) Comfortable ground floor and first floor rooms decorated in old-fashioned French style. More modern-style rooms in the converted attics. The restaurant is decorated with hunting trophies and the food and service is excellent. Marvellous cooked oysters.

Cake and Coffee Shop in the main street of Plelan le Grande Neat, clean, welcoming, excellent coffee and cakes to die for!

Further Reading

We don't want simply to list the wildlife you might see when travelling through France. We believe it would be more helpful to point you in the right direction, tell you about one or two good areas within each region where you will be sure to see something of interest, and allow you the joy of discovery.

When you're planning your holiday, borrow the books you think will be most useful to you personally from the library. If you like what you find when you get to France, and want to go exploring there again, you can always buy your own books when you get back.

We have to admit to wandering about the French countryside with half a dozen identification books each, packed into rucksacks on our backs. If the thought of this makes your knees go weak, don't worry. It's not essential to carry such a heavy load of research information. One or two books, three at the most, will be more than adequate to help you get the most out of your trip.

A Field Guide to the Birds of Britain and Europe, Peterson, Mountfort and Hollom (Collins). Pocket-sized and not too heavy. For over thirty-five years this has been the bible of European birdwatchers. Constantly updated and totally reliable, its coloured illustrations, maps and authoritative text make it an excellent companion.

Field Guide to the Birds of Britain and Europe, John Gooders

(Larousse). A larger pocket-sized book covering over 480 species with in-depth guides to some of the more difficult species, particularly warblers and birds of prey in flight. Contains useful distribution maps next to every species illustrated.

The Illustrated Flora of Britain and Northern Europe by Marjorie Blamey and Christopher Grey-Wilson (Hodder and Stoughton). Beautiful, rather heavy, definitely not a pocket book, but excellent accurate identification of the 2,000 and more plants you may encounter on your travels.

A Concise Guide to the Flowers of Britain and Europe, Oleg Polunin (OUP). Over a thousand colour photographs. Its pocket-size and soft cover makes it a handy walker's companion.

Trees, Keith Rushforth (Mitchell Beazley). Trees are an essential constituent of the landscape yet, despite their great size, are certainly not studied as often as other plants. This hard cover pocket book is one of a series (the Nature Handbooks). Beautifully illustrated, it gives clear accurate identification of native (and introduced) tree species.

The Trees of Britain and Northern Europe, Alan Mitchell and John Wilkinson (Collins). Pocket-sized, this book has over 1,500 colour illustrations, many painted in their native habitat. It's clear, concise and very readable.

Butterflies, Paul Whalley (Michell Beazley). Another in the Nature Handbook Series. It's full of accurate illustrations and authoritative text on all of the butterflies you are likely to come across in Europe.

A Field Guide to the Insects of Britain and Northern Europe, Michael Chinery (Collins). Essential to amateur and professional alike. Very readable. Over one thousand species accurately pictured. Every bug you are likely to find.

A Field Guide to the Caterpillars of Butterflies and Moths in Britain and Europe, D.J. Carter and B. Hargreaves (Collins). A useful book to have in your rucksack or car. Don't be without it if you want to settle an argument over the identification of a sawfly larva.

A Field Guide to the Dragonflies of Britain, Europe and North Africa, J. d'Aguilar, J.-L. Dommanget and R. Prechat, edited by Robert Brooks, (Collins). An English edition of a book originally written in French and recognised as the best guide on the subject. Wonderfully illustrated with colour photographs, paintings and line drawings. The text is a little heavy, but extremely informative.

A Field Guide to the Reptiles and Amphibians of Britain and Europe, E.N. Arnold and J.A. Burton, (Collins). Over 350 wonderful illustrations by D.W. Ovenden – the best pocket book on the subject.

The Mammals of Britain and Europe, Anders Bjärvall and Staffen Ullström (Christopher Helm). Not a pocket-sized book, but highly recommended nevertheless. Few books exist that give such accurate information or show such excellent illustrations of European mammals.

Collins Field Guide to Fresh Water Life, R. Fitter and R. Manuel (Collins). A knowledgeable guide to wetland ecosystems. Well illustrated with a large number of colour photographs. An excellent read with plenty of useful information.

You would find it difficult, if not impossible, to take all these books with you, especially if travelling by air. There'd be little room for life's essentials – other than, perhaps a corkscrew! With economy of space and weight in mind, we'd have to say the three most essential natural history identification guides would be:-

The Larousse Field Guide to the Birds of Britain and Europe

A Concise Guide to the Flowers of Britain and Europe

Paul Whally's *Butterflies*

With these three for identification and a sketch pad, pencil and camera to record what you see, you will not only enjoy your holiday, but also have tangible evidence of your discoveries.

Practical Information

TOURIST OFFICES

UK
Maison de la France, 178 Piccadilly, London W1J 9AL. Tel 0906 8244123 (premium rate line 60p per minute)

US
Maison de la France,
444 Madison Avenue, 16th floor, New York NY 10022. Tel 212-838-7800. Fax 212-838-7855. nypress @francetourism.com

Head Office for Brittany
Comité Régional de Tourisme de Bretagne, 1 rue Raoul Ponchon, 35069 Rennes CEDEX. Tel 33 299 28 44 30. Fax 33 299 28 44 40

Côtes d'Armor
Comité Départemental du Tourisme de Côtes d'Armor, BP 4620, 22046 Saint Brieuc CEDEX 2.

Tel 33 2 96 62 72 00. Fax 33 2 96 33 59 1

Finistère
Comité Départemental du Tourisme de Finistère , BP 29104 Quimper CEDEX. Tel 33 2 98 76 20 70. Fax 33 2 98 52 19 19

Ille et Vilaine
Comité Départemental du Tourisme d'Ile et Vilaine, BP 6046-35060 Rennes CEDEX 3. Tel 33 2 99 78 47 47. Fax 33 2 99 78 33 24

Morbihan
Comité Départemental du Tourisme de Morbihan, Allée Nicolas Leblanc BP 408 56010 Vannes CEDEX. Tel 33 2 97 54 17 12. Fax 33 2 97 42 71 02

CONSERVATION ORGANISATIONS

Service des Espaces Naturels des Conseils Généraux
Hôtel du Département, Côtes d'Armor, 11 Place du Général de Gaulle, 22023 Saint Brieuc CEDEX 01. Tel 02 96 62 27 77

Finistère
32 bd Dupleix, 29196 Quimper CEDEX. Tel 02 98 76 20 20

Ille et Vilaine
1 Avenue de la Préfecture, 35020 Rennes CEDEX. Tel 02 99 02 35 35

Morbihan
Rue Saint-Tropex, 59 009 Vannes CEDEX. Tel 02 97 54 80 00

Conseil Régional de Bretagne
Direction de l'Environnement et du Tourisme, 283 Avenue du Général Patton, 35000 Rennes. Tel 02 99 27 10 10

Direction Régionale de l'Environnement
Les Magister, 6 Cours Raphaël Binet, 35000 Rennes. Tel 02 99 65 35 36

Conservatoire de l'Espace Littoral et des Rivages Lacustres
Port du Légue, 8 Quai Gabriel Péri, 22194 Plerin. Tel 02 96 33 66 32

Conservatoire Botanique National de Brest
52 Allée du Bot, 29200 Brest. Tel 02 98 41 88 95

Office National des Forêts (ONF)
211 rue de Fougeres, 35 019 Rennes CEDEX 7. Tel 02 99 27 47 27

Parc Naturel Régional d'Armorique
15 Place aux Foires, 29 590 Le Faou. Tel 02 98 81 90 08

Société pour l'Etude et la Protection de la Nature en Bretagne (SEPNB) Bretagne Vivante
186 rue Anatole France, 29 200 Brest. Tel 02 98 49 07 18

Ligue pour la Protection des Oiseaux (LPO)
Station Ornithologique de l'Ile Grande, 22 560 Pleumeur-Bodou. Tel 02 96 91 91 40

GETTING THERE

By Air

Direct flights from London to Dinard by Ryanair. Tel 01279 666200

Air France (Britair) – London Gatwick to Nantes/Brest. Tel 0845 084 5222. Fax 01293 507 182

Air France (Britair) – London City Airport to Rennes. Tel 0845 084 5111. Fax 020 8782 8551

British Airways London Gatwick to Nantes. Tel 0845 773 3377. Fax 0161 247 5707

The main US Airlines all fly direct to Charles de Gaulle Airport, Paris from a wide variety of US airports. There are flights into Orly, Paris, and connecting flights from Charles de Gaulle and Orly, Paris to Brest, Rennes and Lorient. Flights to Quimper are from Orly only.

If you are travelling from the US to England, then onward to France, there are quite a number of flights to the French regions from London-Stansted airport; namely Brest, Caen, Dinard and Nantes

For further information on flights from the US, visit: us.franceguide.com/airlines.asp

By car

Condor Ferries from Weymouth to St Malo/Poole to St Malo. Tel 01305 761555

Brittany Ferries from Portsmouth to Caen/Portsmouth to St Malo/Poole to Cherbourg/Poole to St Malo/Plymouth to Roscoff. Tel 08705 360360

P & O Ferries from Portsmouth to Cherbourg. Tel 0870 242 4999. Fax 01705 864211

Le Shuttle (Eurotunnel) from Folkestone (Ashford) to Calais (Sangatte). Tel 08705 353535

Motoring in France You will need :
A valid, full driving licence
Current insurance certificate
Vehicle Registration Document
(a letter of authority from
the owner if the vehicle is
not your own)
GB sticker
Spare set of bulbs
Fire extinguisher
First aid kit
Warning triangle
Headlamp beam deflectors
(yellow lamps are not a
legal requirement)

Insurance Your own policy provides third Party cover throughout Europe.

You may need a Green Card Certificate if you wish to maintain your comprehensive cover – check with your own insurance company.

If you are travelling from the US, you should apply to an insurance company that deals with cases of illness or accident in France.

Speed limits: Towns 50 kph* (31 mph) or lower if indicated; **main roads** 90 kph* (55 mph); **dual carriageways** 110 kph* (68 mph); **motorways** 130 kph* (80 mph)

*In rain or bad weather these limits are reduced by 10 kph (or to 110 kph on motorways).

Seat belts Must be worn.

Drinking & driving The blood alcohol limit is lower than in the UK. In addition, the police have the right to make random breath tests.

Road signs Most international road signs will be instantly recognisable.

The main difference is the priority rule. While major junctions and roundabouts now follow the interntional convention, the 'priority from the right' principle still exists in most towns.

By train

From the UK: take the Eurostar from London, Waterloo to Paris, Gare du Nord, (tel 0870 160 6600, www.eurostar.com) and then take the Metro from Gare du Nord to Monparnasse. Pick up the TGV to Brest, Rennes, Quimper. Change onto local lines to final destination, tel 0870 160 6600, www.tgv.com).

GENERAL INFORMATION

Passports & visas A valid full passport is required for entry into France. No visa is required for citizens of the UK or Irish Republic.

A valid US passport is required. No visa is needed for American visitors staying less than 90 days. For further information on entry requirements into France from the US, visit: us.franceguide.com/practicalentryrequirements.asp

French customs For up to date information on customs visitors from the UK should contact the French Tourist office in London. Visitors from the US should contact the French Tourist Office in New York, or visit www.info-france-usa.org.

Health & medical insurance No special vaccinations are required for France for British travellers.

Medical assistance can be obtained through a reciprocal arrangement with the UK (Form E111) obtainable in advance from your local DHSS Office or post office. In practice, however, we would advise taking out adequate medical insurance as E111 does not provide full cover – being dependent on the treatment and medicines supplied – and only a percentage of your outlay will be reimbursed. Most French people pay into a 'Mutual' on a monthly basis to provide for this difference. If your country of origin does not have a reciprocal arrangement you must ensure that you have proper insurance cover.

Time French time is one hour ahead of Greenwich Mean Time and moves forward a further hour in late March until the end of September. France is therefore one hour ahead throughout the year except for a short period in October before British Summer Time ends.

Public holidays Many public and religious holidays differ from those in UK and other countries and you should bear this in mind when making holiday plans. The holiday is usually celebrated on the actual day of the week on which it falls – although if this is over the weekend, many workers will take the Friday or Monday off.

New Year 1st Jan
Easter Sun & Mon only
Labour Day 1st May
VE Day 8th May
Ascension Day 10 days
  before Whit Sunday

Whitsun Sun & Mon
(6 weeks after Easter)
Bastille/National Day
14th July
Assumption Day 15th Aug
All Saints Day 1st Nov
Armistice Day 11th Nov
Christmas 25th Dec only

Post offices In addition to the usual post office services you will also be able to send faxes. Most post offices also have a Minitel set – an interactive teletext system which provides a wealth of information and booking facilities and can be used for directory enquiries. This service is activated by dialling '11' followed by the green ENVOI button. The first three minutes are free with a small charge thereafter.

Many of the larger post offices have useful machines that supply not only books of stamps, but single stamps, which means you don't get stuck with a lot of stamps you can't use. (*Tabacs* also sell stamps for postcards.) And of course, there is a fast growing number of cyber cafes.

Banks & currency Your local high street bank, exchange bureaux, travel agency and the ferry companies can all provide French currency before you arrive in France. Once there you will also be able to exchange currency and travellers cheques at banks displaying the change sign. Many hotels also offer this service, but

it's often more expensive. Most credit cards are widely accepted in shops, supermarkets and restaurants and Visa cards can be used to obtain currency at hole in the wall dispensers (often with the instructions in English.)

The currency in France, since January 2002, is the Euro.

Disabled travellers The French Tourist Office in London can supply a list of companies able to accommodate disabled clients. For further information contact the French Tourist Office, Maison de la France, 178 Piccadilly, London W1V OAL. Tel 0906 8244123 (this is a premium rate line at 60p per minute).

Maps Most people who have travelled by car in France before will have their own favourite general map. But if you haven't, The Leisure Map of France & Belgium, published by Estate Publications is the one we use to get around. It's clear and easy to read. Once you've reached your destination, it's useful to have a more detailed map. For Brittany Carte Routière et Touristique Michelin no. 230 is a good one; another is The Globe-trotter Travel Map of Brittany.

Local tourist offices will have more specific maps and are happy to help with any queries.

Electricity supply In France the supply is 220 volts and a two-pin adaptor is necessary.

WHAT TO DO

Cycling Organised cycling holidays are available if you're not sure about taking off on your own. Bicycles, maps and a full itinerary are provided to guide you from hotel to hotel so that you may pedal along the country lanes while your baggage is taken on ahead. For information contact Maison de la France in London or relevant Tourist Offices in France (see p. 189).

Walking The whole of France is laced with a network of public footpaths called Randonnées. The Petites Randonnées – 'PR Paths' – are usually circular trails of 2 to 6 hours walking, or day hikes for experienced ramblers. Grande Randonnées – 'GR or 'GPR' – are long distance footpaths, which take several days to complete and are either circular, or from A to B. No cars are allowed on these paths. All the footpaths are marked with red and white, or yellow and red, or single yellow lines – often half way up a wall, or on the trunk of a tree (so you need to look carefully for them.) 'Straight On' is shown by a combination of horizontal lines. 'Change of Direction' is shown by a right angle pointing in the direction to be taken. A cross indicates 'No Entry' – or 'Don't go this way.'

Sometimes the footpaths run through farmyards and along the bottom of gardens. A polite 'bonjour' to the farmer or householder will usually elicit a friendly response – and often an invitation to buy home-grown produce – apples, cherries and strawberries in season.

For full details on the Randonnée network contact FFRP (Fédération Française de la Randonnée Pedestre) located at 14 rue Riquet – 75919 Paris, or log on to the excellent Brittany Tourist website: www.tourismebretagne.com.

All the local tourist offices in France, even in small towns and villages, will be able to advise on walks in their region and often supply maps, free of charge.

Inland boating Motor cruisers and *pénichets* (specially designed river boats) from two to twelve berth can be hired and motored along an extensive network of rivers, including the rivers Vilaine, Rance and the Nantes–Brest Canal. There are also many organised, 'guided' river trips. For further information, contact Maison de la

France in London or the relevant local tourist offices in France (see p. 191).

Coastal boating Naturally all the major seaside towns run boat trips to places of interest. It's best to apply to the local tourist office for further information (see p. 191).

Water sports Brittany has a splendid long coastline with a great many seaside resorts (large and small) – most of them providing facilities for all sorts of water sports. The local tourist offices will have all the information you need about what is on offer and where to find it.

Special interest holidays Many companies organise special interest holidays in France: riding; driving horse-drawn caravans along country lanes; canoeing; golf; thalassotherapy (a form of health treatment based on sea water and natural marine products); boating; walking; cycling; gastronomy (eating!); cooking; visiting wine caves; and historical tours.

You can either join an organised tour with a guide, or be more independent. For further information contact the French Tourist Office in London, or the relevant local tourist offices in France (see p. 191).

SUGGESTED TOUR OF BRITTANY

Leave St Malo and cross the barrage over the Rance Estuary. Pick up the D168 heading towards Ploubalay, Matignon and Fréhel. The coast here is deeply indented with plenty of places to stop and look at the fauna and flora, which is typical of salt marsh. As you get closer to Cap Fréhel itself, the land rises steeply, forming thrift-topped cliffs full of seabirds in the breeding season.

From Cap Fréhel the coast road runs through Plurien and on to Cap d'Erquy – it's a green route and quite lovely. The Cap is a well-known spot for migrants. Black redstarts breed along the cliffs and in spring wheatears display on the top of the thyme-covered ant hills. There are also spotted orchids in the folds of the cliff top. Continue on this road towards Pléneuf Val André (the beaches along this part of the coast are highly recommended) and on to Langueux where you can choose either to pick up the E50 to Guincamp, then the D767 to Lannion and the D788 to Perros Guirec and the boat trip to Les Sept Iles. Or you can potter along the D786 that keeps closer to the coast, taking a boat trip to Ile de Bréhat, then, still on the D786, cross to Tréguier – coming to Les Sept Iles in a more leisurely fashion. We believe Les Sept Iles is a must because it is such an incredible area for seabirds, particularly in the breeding season with puffins and gannets and the possibility of seeing seals.

From Les Sept Iles take the road back to Lannion, then the D786 to Morlaix. Pick up the E50 for a short distance then turn off onto the D785 to Roc'h Trevezel and Pleyben. The D785 eventually joins the E60 to Quimper. This road takes you right through the Parc d'Armorique and over the highlands of the Monts d'Arrée. If you have the time, or inclination, branch off at Roc'h Trevezel onto the D764 to Huelgoat. This area boasts wonderful ancient woodlands and deep mossy rock-filled gorges – excellent habitat for birds of prey, dragonflies and woodland butterflies such as white admiral.

Quimper itself is well worth exploration, especially the old quarter. A centre for ceramics, there are many really good examples of typical Breton tableware to be found and the lovely cathedral of St Corentin should not be missed.

Leaving Quimper and heading towards the south Finistère coast, take the D34 to Bénodet, an excellent base to explore this part of the Côte de Cornouaille, also known as the Pays Bigoudin. From Bénodet, cross the bridge heading towards Pont l'Abbé on the D44 and very soon you will come to a sign marked Kermor Plage. This lovely wide beach is backed by a nature reserve and a substantial sand martin colony in the wind-cut face of the beach dunes. In the other direction from Bénodet, heading towards Fouesnant on the D44, look for signs to Pointe de Mousterlin. Behind the rocky coastline lies an area of degraded dunes, rich in typical dune plants like marram and marsh mallow and fennel, the latter being the food plant for swallowtail butterflies. There are also sand lizards. It's a good place for a picnic.

For a little historical interest carry on to Concarneau and Pont Aven. You can either take the E60 (165) main route from Quimper for speed, or you can follow the smaller D763 to Concarneau and then the D24 from Concarneau to Pont Aven. The original walled town of Concarneau sits in the harbour and is reached by a short stone causeway, a drawbridge and a fortified town gate. Although popular with tourists and rather crowded in high summer, it is a charming place and you should try to fit in a visit if you can. Pont Aven is an artist's town with a scatter of wonderful old mills running down the hill alongside the river.

Paul Gauguin lived and painted here and many of the old mill buildings have been converted into art galleries or restaurants.

Depending on how much time you have, you can travel back to St Malo by a completely different route, taking in a whole new set of landscapes and wildlife.

Saying goodbye to southern Finistère, travel on to the Golfe du Morbihan, stopping at Carnac on the way. From Quimper take the E60 to Auray and turn off onto the D768 to Plouharnel and then onto the D781 to Carnac and the Museum of Prehistory. Here you will see the fantastic stone alignments dating from the late Stone Age and covering hundred of acres. You simply cannot visit this part of France and not see the stones at Carnac. It would be a crime.

The most straightforward way of getting from Carnac to the Golfe du Morbihan and Presqu'île du Rhuys is to head back to Auray and the E60 to Vannes. Watch carefully for the sign to Séné, a substantial nature reserve with avocets, black-tailed godwits, common terns and black-winged stilts. The hides are well positioned to give a good view of the whole reserve. Back up to the E60 again and turn onto the D780 towards Sarzeau. This takes you alongside the Golfe du Morbihan and the Office de Tourisme is very helpful in pointing you in the right direction for whatever it is you might be interested in – whether it is historic buildings, beaches or nature reserves.

Retrace your steps to Vannes and take the 166 heading towards Ploërmel. Take the ring road until you see the sign for Campénéac and Plélan le Grand (where there is an excellent coffee and cake shop in the main high street). Look for the D733 to Paimpont – right in the centre of the Fôret de Brocéliande (otherwise known as the Fôret Domaniale de Paimpont.) The town of Paimpont itself is a good base for the whole area. The woodlands here are very ancient and dotted with hammer ponds. It is a centre for hunting with wild boar, fallow and roe deer and large numbers and species of birds of prey, including goshawks and honey buzzards. Excellent too for golden orioles.

On the way back to St Malo and the ferry take the D773 to Gaël, then the 166 heading towards St Meen le Grand and the 766 to Dinan. Try to make time to explore this lovely old city and, of course, do try to take time to have a good look around St Malo itself. Too often we simply get on or off the ferry and drive somewhere else. But St Malo is well worth further exploration.

Like a phoenix it has risen from the ashes. During the Second World War it was occupied by the Germans and in 1944 bombarded by the Allies leaving 80% of the walled city in ruins. In 1948 an inspired town council and determined population began rebuilding and restoration; and within five years the lovely granite architecture, including the mansions of the Corsairs, looked just as it had done in the 16th and 17th centuries.

MARKET DAYS

Local markets are one of the best ways of exploring a region's special character – and to stock up on picnic goods.

* Denotes seasonal markets only (July and August)

**Denotes seasonal market every day from April to September

Côtes d'Armor

	Mon	Tues	Wed	Thurs	Fri	Sat	Sun
Bégard					Fri		
Belle Isle en Terre			Wed				
Binic				Thurs	Fri*		
Broons			Wed				
Bourbriac		Tues					
Callac			Wed				
Caulnes		Tues					
Châtelaudren	Mon						
Dinan				Thurs			
Erqy						Sat	
Etables sur Mer		Tues				Sat*	
Fréhel		Tues					
Guimcamp					Fri	Sat	
Jugon les Lacs					Fri		
Lamballe				Thurs			
Lancieux		Tues*					
Lannion				Thurs			
Lanvollon					Fri		
Lézardrieux					Fri		
Louargat				Thurs			
Loudéac						Sat	
Louguivy-Plougras					Fri		
Matignon			Wed				
Merdignac			Wed				
Moncontour	Mon						
Mûr de Bretagne					Fri (eves)*		
Paimpol		Tues					
Penvenan						Sat	
Perret							Sun*
Perros-Guirec					Fri		
Plancoët						Sat	
Planguenoual	Mon*						
Plédran						Sat	
Pléneuf		Tues					

	Mon	Tues	Wed	Thurs	Fri	Sat	Sun
Pléneuf Val André					Fri*		
Plérin							Sun
Plestin les Grèves		Tues (eves)*					Sun
Pleubian						Sat	
Plouaret		Tues					
Ploubalay					Fri		
Plouec sur Lié				Thurs			
Plouezec						Sat	
Ploufragan-Plurien					Fri*		
Plouha			Wed				
Ploumilliau						Sat	
Pontrieux	Mon						
Pordic					Fri		
La Roche Derrien					Fri		
Rostrenen		Tues					
Quintin		Tues					
St Brieuc			Wed			Sat	Sun
St Cast le Guildo	Mon*				Fri		
St Jacut de la Mer					Fri		
St Michel en Grève	Mon						
St Quay Portrieux	Mon				Fri		
Taden					Fri (eves)*		
Trébeurden		Tues					
Trégastel	Mon						
Trégueux					Fri		
Tréguier			Wed				

Finistère

	Mon	Tues	Wed	Thurs	Fri	Sat	Sun
Audierne						Sat	
Bannalec			Wed (2nd and 4th of the month)				
Bénodet	Mon						
Brasparts	Mon (1st of the month)						
Brest	Mon	Tues	Wed	Thurs	Fri	Sat	Sun
Briec					Fri		
Briec		Tues (1st of the month)					
Brignognan Plages					Fri*		
Camaret sur Mer {	Mon*		Wed*	Thurs*	Fri*	Sat*	Sun*
		Tues (3rd of the month)					
Carantec				Thurs			
Carhaix						Sat	
Châteaulin*				Thurs			Sun*
Châteauneuf du Faou			Wed (1st, 3rd & 5th of the month)				

203

	Mon	Tues	Wed	Thurs	Fri	Sat	Sun
Cléden Cap Sizun				Thurs (4th of the month)			
Cléder					Fri		Sun*
Clohars-Carnoët						Sat	
Combrit			Wed				
Concarneau	Mon				Fri		
Crozon			Wed (2nd and 4th of the month)				
Daoulas							Sun
Dinéault		Tues			Fri		
Douarnenez	Mon		Wed			Sat	
Ergué-Gabéric		Tues (3rd of the month)					
Fouesnant les Glénan					Fri		
Guerlesquin	Mon						
Guilers					Fri		
Guipavas					Fri		
Huelgoat				Thurs			
Ile d'Ouessant			Wed			Sat	
Ile Tudy	Mon*						
Kerhuon						Sat	
L'Hôpital-Camfrout					Fri		
La Forêt-Fouesnant		Tues (eves)*					Sun
Lampaul–Plouarzel				Thurs			
Landéda		Tues					
Landerneau		Tues			Fri	Sat	
Landivisiau			Wed				
Lanmeur					Fri		
Lannilis			Wed				
Le Conquet		Tues					
Le Faou		Tues				Sat (last of the month)	
Le Guilvinec		Tues				Sat	Sun*
Le Relecq						Sat	
Lesneven	Mon						
Locmaria-Plouzané				Thurs			
Locquirec			Wed				
Loctudy		Tues					
Melgven						Sat	
Moëlan sur Mer		Tues					
Morlaix			Wed			Sat	
Névez						Sat	
Pleyben		Tues (2nd of the month)				Sat	
Plobannalec-Lesconil			Wed				
Plogoff					Fri		
Plogonnec						Sat	
Plomodiern					Fri (1st of the month)		

	Mon	Tues	Wed	Thurs	Fri	Sat	Sun
Plonéour-Lanvern					Fri (last of the month)		
Plonévez du Faou					Fri (2nd of the month)		
Ploudalmézeau					Fri		
Plouescat						Sat	
Plougasnou		Tues					
Plougastel-Daoulas				Thurs			
Plougonvelin							Sun*
Plouguerneau				Thurs			
Plouguerneau-Lilia		Tues (eves)*					
Plougonven		Tues					
Plouhinec							Sun*
Plouigneau							Sun
Plounéour-Trez				Thurs*			
Plouzané			Wed				
Plozévet	Mon (1st of the month)						
Pont Aven		Tues					
Pont l'Abbé				Thurs			
Pont Croix				Thurs			
Primelin				Thurs*			
Riec sur Belon			Wed				
Rosporden				Thurs			
Quimper			Wed		Fri (eves)	Sat	Sun
Quimperlé					Fri		
Riec sur Belon						Sat	
Roscoff			Wed				
Santec						Sat	Sun*
Scaër						Sat	
Sizun					Fri (1st of the month)		
Spézet					Fri (last of the month)		
St Guénolé					Fri		
St Martin des Champs							Sun
St Nic sur Pentrez	Daily**						
St Pol de Léon		Tues					
St Renan						Sat	
Telgruc sur Mer		Tues			Fri		
Treffiagat						Sat	
Trégourez					Fri (3rd of the month)		
Trégunc		Tues	Wed (eves)				Sun*

Ille et Vilaine

	Mon	Tues	Wed	Thurs	Fri	Sat	Sun
Acigné			Wed				
Antrain		Tues					
Argentré du Plessis				Thurs			
Bain de Bretagne	Mon						
Bazouges la Pérouse				Thurs			
Beaucé – Bruz					Fri		
Bécherel						Sat	
Bédée						Sat	
Betton							Sun
Bréal sous Montfort						Sat	
Cancale							Sun
Cesson-Sévigné						Sat	
Chartres de Bretagne				Thurs			
Châteaubourg					Fri		
Châteaugiron				Thurs			
Chavagne			Wed				
Combourg	Mon						
Corps-Nuds			Wed				
Dinard		Tues		Thurs		Sat	
Dol de Bretagne						Sat	
Fougères				Thurs		Sat	
Gaël					Fri		
Goven			Wed				
Guichen		Tues					
Guignen			Wed				
Guipry				Thurs			
Hédé		Tues					
Iffendic						Sat	
Irodouer					Fri		
Janzé			Wed				
L'Hermitage						Sat	
La Bouexière						Sat	
La Chapelle des Fougeretz						Sat	
La Guerche de Bretagne		Tues					
La Mézière							Sun
La Richardais							Sun
Langouet				Thurs			
Le Grand Fougeray						Sat	
Le Petre			Wed				
Le Rheu						Sat	
Lécousse							Sun
Liffré					Fri		

	Mon	Tues	Wed	Thurs	Fri	Sat	Sun
Lohéac						Sat	
Louvigné du Désert					Fri		
Martigné-Ferchaud					Fri		
Maure de Bretagne							Sun
Melesse				Thurs			
Miniac-Morvan					Fri		
Monfort sur Meu					Fri		
Montauban de Bretagne			Wed				
Mordelles		Tues					
Noyal sur Vilaine		Tues					
Noyal Châtillon sur Seiche							Sun
Pacé			Wed				
Pipriac		Tues					
Plélan le Grand							Sun
Pleine-Fougères		Tues					
Plerguer			Wed				
Pleurtuit					Fri		
Redon	Mon						
Rennes		Tues	Wed	Thurs	Fri	Sat	
Retiers						Sat	
Saint Ouen des Alleux			Wed				
Sens de Bretagne	Mon						
Servon sur Vilaine							Sun
St Aubin d'Aubigné		Tues					
St Aubin du Cormier				Thurs			
St Briac	Mon*				Fri	Sat*	
St Brice en Coglès				(2nd of the month)			Sun
St Domineuc						Sat	
St Georges de Reintembault				Thurs			
St Gilles						Sat	
St Grégoire			Wed				
St Lunaire							Sun*
St Malo	Mon	Tues	Wed	Thurs	Fri	Sat	
St Médard sur Ille						Sat	
St Méen le Grand						Sat	
St Méloir des Ondes				Thurs			
Thorigné-Fouillard							Sun
Tinténiac			Wed				
Trans				Thurs			
Vern sur Seiche						Sat	
Vitré	Mon						

Morbihan

	Mon	Tues	Wed	Thurs	Fri	Sat	Sun
Ambon							Sun*
Arradon		Tues			Fri		
Arzon		Tues					
Auray	Mon						
Baden							Sun
Baud			Wed (1st of the month)			Sat	
Béganne – Carnac							Sun
Bubry			Wed (2nd & 4th of the month)				
Carentoir		Tues (1st of the month)					
Carnac			Wed				
Caudan		Tues					
Cléguérec			Wed (eves)*				
Crec'h				Thurs			
Damgan		Tues*				Sat*	
Elven					Fri		
Erdeven	Mon (eves)*						
Etel		Tues					
Gourin	Mon						
Grandchamp					Fri (1st of the month)		
Guéméné sur Scorff				Thurs			
Guer			Wed				
Guidel					Fri*(eves)		Sun
Guilliers		Tues					
Hennebont				Thurs			
Ile aux Moines					Fri		
Josselin						Sat	
Kervoyal			Wed*				
La Faouët			Wed (1st & 3rd of the month)				
La Gacilly						Sat	
La Roche Bernard				Thurs			
La Trinité sur Mer		Tues			Fri		
La Trinité Porhoët	Mon (2nd of the month)						
Lanester		Tues					
Languidic					Fri		
Larmor-Baden							Sun
Larmor-Plage		Tues (eves, once a fortnight)*					Sun
Le Bono						Sat	
Le Palais		Tues			Fri		
Le Roc St André							Sun
Locmaria							Sun

	Mon	Tues	Wed	Thurs	Fri	Sat	Sun
Locmariaquer		Tues				Sat	
Locminé				Thurs			
Locmiquelic					Fri		
Lorient			Wed			Sat	
Malansac		Tues					
Malestroit				Thurs			
Mauron					Fri		
Muzillac					Fri		Sun
Noyal							Sun
Pénestin			Wed*				Sun
Plescop						Sat	Sun
Ploemeur			Wed*(eves)				Sun
Ploërmel	Mon				Fri		
Ploeren							Sun
Plouay						Sat	
Plougoumelen					Fri		
Plouhinec							Sun
Pluvigner		Tues (2nd of the month)					
Pontivy	Mon						
Pont Scorff						Sat	
Port Crouesty	Mon*						
Port Louis		Tues*(eves)				Sat	
Port Navalo					Fri*		
Questembert	Mon						
Queven							Sun
Quiberon						Sat	
Riantec			Wed				
Sarzeau				Thurs			
Sauzon				Thurs			
Sené					Fri		
Sérent			Wed				
Ste Anne d'Auray			Wed				
St Ave							Sun
St Gildas de Rhuys							Sun
St Jean Brévelay		Tues (1st & 3rd of the month)					
St Philibert					Fri		
St Pierre Quiberon				Thurs			
St Servant Surzur							Sun
Theix							Sun
Vannes			Wed			Sat	Sun

Acknowledgements

A lot of work goes into writing a book and in the creation of this series we have been fortunate indeed in the help and support we've received from so many people, individuals and organisations, in France and in England. It is impossible to name them all. To these unnamed people who freely shared their experience and knowledge of the region – the wines, restaurants and local specialties – we give a vote of thanks.

On our many trips to the Western Loire region and the Vendée, writing for the French Tourist Office we had, naturally, to travel through parts of Brittany, but it was several years before we had the opportunity to do more than take a fleeting look. We were always promising ourselves we would stop for a few days, but we never did. That is until we met the Brittany Tourist Office people one dull, drizzly November day at a workshop in London. Their enthusiasm and description of the delights to be found in Brittany reinforced our own somewhat limited impressions – and we were on our way. We would like to thank the directors and staff at the Comité Régional du Tourisme Bretagne, based in the ancient city of Rennes for providing invaluable help and advice. The departmental tourist offices too, were always ready with suggestions, information leaflets and maps. Côtes d'Armor, Finistère, Ille et Vilaine and the little local tourist office on the Presqu'île du Rhuys which serves the area of the Golfe du Morbihan.

We must also express our obligation to the Press and Public

Affairs Department of Maison de la France at 178 Piccadilly in London. They are always supportive and direct us towards just the right person we need to see or to speak to in France.

The conservation movement in France is still in its youth, but therein lies its strength, and interest in natural history is expanding rapidly, thanks largely to increased information available from conservation organisations, particularly the LPO (Ligue pour la Protection des Oiseaux). We are grateful to Alison Duncan, an Englishwoman, married to a Frenchman, and her small but dedicated staff who are unfailingly helpful. We first crossed to Brittany with Brittany Ferries many years ago when the service was far less developed than it is today and have fond recollections of enjoyable crossings to Caen (Ouisteram) and to Cherbourg on the Cotentin Peninsula (both ports actually in Normandy) and also to the beautiful port of St Malo in Brittany itself. They are now one of the major passenger carriers with a fleet of modern car ferries, but they still retain that feeling of being in France from the moment you step aboard. We'd like to thank Toby Oliver and his staff who are always helpful.

We have used practically every conventional means of crossing the English Channel during our many trips to France and the speed and quality of service provided by Condor Ferries, one of the newer cross Channel carriers who use high-speed, wave-piercing catamarans dramatically and pleasurably shortening the journey time between Poole or Weymouth and St Malo, is always impressive and we're grateful to Nick Dobbs and the Directors, cabin staff and crew for their friendliness and attention to safety.

Bovey Tracy Hand Loom Weavers in Devon produce excellent tweed cloth and, as we come from Devon, it seemed only right to have some made into jackets, suits and caps. We've been wearing clothes made from their cloth for more than two decades and are pleased to do so. However, as warm and comfortable as tweed is during the autumn and winter, especially when you're tramping through the countryside, it is not really practical for summer wear and this is where Orvis comes in. An American company based in Andover, they make lighter, less formal, equally comfortable country-style clothes and specialise in umpteen hidden pockets – ideal for travelling – and we rely on Ruth Ryan for suggestions.

Last, but not least, thank you to Mandy Little and Sugra Zaman, directors of Watson Little, our agents who have been extremely active on our behalf. And our publishers, Alexander Fyjis-Walker and Ava Li of Pallas Athene for their understanding and creativity.

About the Authors

Naturalist and broadcaster Dennis Furnell was born in London, spent his childhood in the West Country, and began his natural history career with the RSPB film unit in 1956. He has been involved with national and international conservation ever since, broadcasting for the past 21 years on BBC and Independent Radio and on BBC television, Channel 4 and The Discovery Channel, as well as producing and presenting Nature's Way for Anglia TV. He was also instrumental in helping to set up the Visual Language Media Group, a television training facility for people with hearing impairment. Ann Furnell, born in Brixham, Devon is a researcher and editor.

Now living in Hertfordshire, together they have written seven books and more than one million words in commissioned feature articles. Married for 40 years, with one son, Robin, daughter-in-law Natalie and two grand-daughters, Yasmin and Isla, they are enthusiastic travellers with diverse interests, and have led several natural history holidays in Europe.

First introduced to France a little over 30 years ago by friends who lived in the Auvergne, they were captivated by this lovely country and its incredible wildlife. They are currently working on the third book in the Nature of France series – wanting to communicate their fascination and delight in the landscape, history, culture, food and wine.

Index

PALLAS ATHENE

The Nature of France
Western Loire and Vendée
Dennis and Ann Furnell

The second book in the series *The Nature of France, Western Loire and the Vendée,* takes us through the reed-fringed waterways of the Brière, one of France's best kept natural history secrets – an area of wetland second only in size to the Carmargue, and home to a breathtaking diversity of wildlife. Discover avocets and black kites, marsh harriers and dragonflies, where the paludiers skim the fleurs de sel (flowers of salt) from the salt pans on the Presqu'île Guérandaise. And sample dishes as intriguing as 'eels in roquefort' in a tiny Brièron restaurant, or explore the Belle Epoque grandeur of the region's capital, Nantes.

The coastline boasts miles and miles of golden sands, as well as salt-pans and mud flats that are paradise for myriad waders. To the south, the land is laced with thousands of kilometres of tree-fringed canals dug by monks and peasants during the middle ages. Nightingales and warblers sing, and crickets and frogs add a wonderful background to a picnic of fresh baked bread and cheese washed down with Brem, the local red wine.

The Furnells are unashamedly Francophiles. They will help you to discover a side of France often missed by other guide books – and bring out the true Nature of France.

224 pp all in colour, durable binding ISBN 1 873429 86 X £12.99 Spring 2004

PALLAS ATHENE

Other books on France from Pallas Athene

DORDOGNE
JOY LAW
The best sort of travel book Spectator
ISBN 1 873429 86 X   £14.99

PROVENCE
MICHAEL JACOBS
The ideal companion we all dream of Irish Independent
ISBN 1 873429 86 X   £15.99

MIDI
JOY LAW
Required reading TLS
ISBN 1 873429 86 X   £15.99

AN HOUR FROM PARIS
ANNABEL SIMMS
Groundbreaking stuff *The Sunday Times*
ISBN 1 873429 86 X   £12.99

THE GENEROUS EARTH
PHILIP OYLER
The great classic of peasant life in the Dordogne,
first published in 1950
ISBN 1 873429 86 X   £12.99

Cover: Gorse *(Ulex europaeus)* and Heather/Ling:
Gorse is extremely important on marginal heathland.
The root system traps nitrogen in the soil maintaining
fertility in otherwise sterile conditions and the
brilliant flowers bloom all year round
Frontispiece: Pointe de Mousterlin, Finistère: The tide rip between
the rocky outcrop is dramatic at all stages of the tide.
Cormorants and shags fish in the turbulent waters
Contents pages: small

All photographs, watercolour paintings and
pencil drawings by Dennis Furnell except:
pp. 131, 135 photo: Gratien, Brittany Tourist Office

Text copyright © Dennis & Ann Furnell 2003
The moral right of the
authors has been asserted

Published 2003 by
Pallas Athene (Publishers) Ltd
59 Linden Gardens
London W2 4HJ
WWW.PALLASATHENE.CO.UK

Series Editor: Alexander Fyjis-Walker
Editor: Ava Li
Design Consultant: James Sutton
Maps by Ted Hammond,
except back inside cover, courtesy of FFRP

ISBN 1 873429 89 4

Printed in China
through World Print Ltd

LONG DISTANCE FOOTPATHS IN BRITTANY (

Paimpol

16 Lannion

1

Morlaix

4 Guingamp

5 PNR St-Brie

13 Brest d'ARMORIQUE

Huelgoat **7**

Le Faou Carhaix

11

Crozon LAC de GUERLEDAN Lou

POINTE du RAZ **9**

Quimper Pontivy

10 Concarneau **18**

12 Quimperlé Baud

Lorient

Auray Van

14

Quiberon

Belle-Ile

Signs used on the paths

	GR' Grande Randonnée	GRP' Grande Randonnée de Pays	PR Promenade et Randonnée
Straight on			
Change of direction			
Not this way			